ALPHA ZULU À PORTE-AVIONS POSÉIDON : MISSION TERMINÉE, JE RENTRE À LA MAISON !...

VOUS POUVEZ FAIRE CHAUFFER LE CAFÉ !

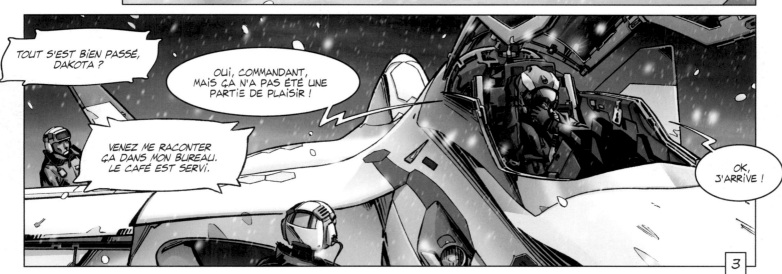

TOUT S'EST BIEN PASSÉ, DAKOTA ?

OUI, COMMANDANT, MAIS ÇA N'A PAS ÉTÉ UNE PARTIE DE PLAISIR !

VENEZ ME RACONTER ÇA DANS MON BUREAU. LE CAFÉ EST SERVI.

OK, J'ARRIVE !

3

BON !... MAINTENANT À TOI DE JOUER, MON GROS PÉPÈRE, JE TE PASSE LES COMMANDES !

JE NE SUIS PAS GROS !... JE SUIS, AU CONTRAIRE, LE PLUS LÉGER ET LE PLUS PERFORMANT DES HÉLICOPTÈRES ACTUELLEMENT EN SERVICE DANS L'EUROPEAN NAVY !

TE VEXE PAS !... JE PLAISANTAIS !... JE T'AI APPELÉ COMME ÇA PARCE QUE JE NE CONNAIS PAS TON MATRICULE !... C'EST QUOI, AU FAIT ?

X27AGS11LT410 !... MAIS LES PILOTES M'APPELLENT GÉNÉRALEMENT PAR MON DIMINUTIF : X 27 !

OK !... MAINTENANT, AU BOULOT !... PRIMO : HÉLITREUILLAGE !... OUVRE LA PORTE LATÉRALE, S'IL TE PLAÎT !

C'EST BON, JE SUIS ACCROCHÉ !... TU PEUX Y ALLER !

5

QUE PRÉVOIT LA MÉTÉO POUR LES HEURES À VENIR ?

AUCUNE AMÉLIORATION AVANT CE SOIR, COMMANDANT.

JE COMMENCE À REGRETTER D'AVOIR LAISSÉ DAKOTA PARTIR SEUL PAR UN TEMPS PAREIL !... S'IL LUI ARRIVAIT QUELQUE CHOSE, JE NE ME LE PARDONNERAIS PAS !

VOUS LE CONNAISSEZ DEPUIS LONGTEMPS ?

DIX ANS !... IL ÉTAIT, À L'ÉPOQUE, LE PLUS JEUNE PILOTE DE L'EUROPEAN AIR FORCE ET DÉJÀ LE PLUS BRILLANT !

"DAKOTA", C'EST SON VÉRITABLE NOM ?

NON, MAIS TOUT LE MONDE OU PRESQUE L'APPELLE COMME ÇA !... C'EST UN SURNOM QUI LUI VIENT DE L'ENFANCE. QUAND IL ÉTAIT GOSSE, IL HABITAIT PRÈS D'UN AÉRODROME. CHAQUE JOUR, APRÈS L'ÉCOLE, IL ALLAIT TRAÎNER AUTOUR DES AVIONS...

ET IL AVAIT FINI PAR SE LIER D'AMITIÉ AVEC UN MÉCANO QUI RESTAURAIT DE VIEUX COUCOUS...

T'AS EU DE BONNES NOTES, AUJOURD'HUI ?

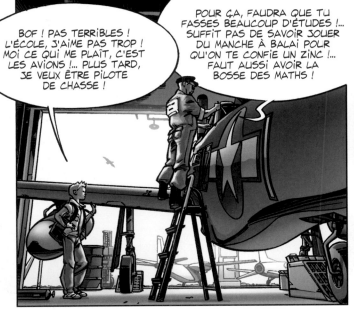

BOF ! PAS TERRIBLES ! L'ÉCOLE, J'AIME PAS TROP ! MOI CE QUI ME PLAÎT, C'EST LES AVIONS !... PLUS TARD, JE VEUX ÊTRE PILOTE DE CHASSE !

POUR ÇA, FAUDRA QUE TU FASSES BEAUCOUP D'ÉTUDES !... SUFFIT PAS DE SAVOIR JOUER DU MANCHE À BALAI POUR QU'ON TE CONFIE UN ZINC !... FAUT AUSSI AVOIR LA BOSSE DES MATHS !

AH BON ?

OUAIS !... C'EST COMME JE TE LE DIS !... ALORS À PARTIR DE MAINTENANT, FAUT QUE T'EN METTES UN COUP À L'ÉCOLE, D'ACCORD !... ET LE JOUR OÙ TU ME RAPPORTERAS UN VINGT SUR VINGT EN CALCUL, PEUT-ÊTRE BIEN QUE JE TE MONTRERAI LE PLUS BEL AVION QUE T'AS JAMAIS VU !

C'EST VRAI ?... OÙ IL EST ?

ON EN RECAUSERA LE MOMENT VENU !... EN ATTENDANT, VA FAIRE TES DEVOIRS !

7

"LES JOURS SUIVANTS, LE PETIT ÉCOLIER NE REVINT PAS. IL NE REPARUT QU'UN MOIS PLUS TARD..."

OÙ T'ÉTAIS PASSÉ ?... ÇA FAIT UNE ÉTERNITÉ QUE JE T'AI PAS VU !... JE CROYAIS QUE TU M'AVAIS OUBLIÉ !

OH NON, JE VOUS AI PAS OUBLIÉ !... AU CONTRAIRE : J'AI FAIT CE QUE VOUS M'AVEZ DIT !

C'EST-À-DIRE ?

BEN, J'AI TRAVAILLÉ DUR À L'ÉCOLE !

VINGT SUR VINGT EN CALCUL !... BRAVO, MON GARÇON, C'EST TRÈS BIEN !

LA MAÎTRESSE NOUS A DONNÉ NOS CARNETS DE NOTES AUJOURD'HUI, ALORS JE VOUS AI APPORTÉ LE MIEN !

BON, ALORS OÙ IL EST ?

QUOI DONC ?

L'AVION QUE VOUS AVEZ PROMIS DE ME MONTRER !

QUEL AVION ?... JE NE VOIS PAS DE QUOI TU PARLES !

MAIS SI !...

MÊME QUE VOUS M'AVEZ DIT QUE C'EST LE PLUS BEAU DU MONDE !

J'AI DIT ÇA, MOI ?... TU ES SÛR ?... C'EST BIZARRE, JE NE M'EN SOUVIENS PLUS !... JE PERDS LA MÉMOIRE, C'EST LA VIEILLESSE !

?!

8

REGARDEZ : LE PUBLIC NOUS APPLAUDIT !

LES BRAVES GENS !... JE VAIS LES SALUER POUR LES REMERCIER, ÇA LEUR FERA PLAISIR !

M... MES LUNETTES !... LE VENT LES A ARRACHÉES !... JE N'Y VOIS PLUS RIEN !... JE NE VAIS PAS POUVOIR POSER LE ZINC !

JE VAIS LE FAIRE À VOTRE PLACE !

TOI ?... T'ES FOU, TU N'AS JAMAIS PILOTÉ DE TA VIE !

?!

IL FAUT BIEN COMMENCER UN JOUR !... DE TOUTE FAÇON, ON N'A PAS LE CHOIX !

TU AS RAISON : C'EST LA SEULE SOLUTION !... BON, JE VAIS T'INDIQUER COMMENT PROCÉDER !

PAS LA PEINE !... JE CONNAIS LE CALEPIN PAR CŒUR !

PENDANT LES CINQ ANS QU'ON A BOSSÉ ENSEMBLE, JE VOUS AI POSÉ DES TAS DE QUESTIONS SUR LE PILOTAGE DE CET AVION. DÈS QUE JE RENTRAIS CHEZ MOI, JE NOTAIS VOS RÉPONSES SUR UN CALEPIN POUR NE PAS LES OUBLIER. ET CHAQUE SOIR, AVANT DE M'ENDORMIR, JE LES RELISAIS PLUSIEURS FOIS POUR BIEN M'EN SOUVENIR.

QUEL CALEPIN ?

10

PARFOIS, QUAND VOUS N'ÉTIEZ PAS LÀ, J'EN PROFITAIS POUR M'ASSEOIR AUX COMMANDES ET JE SIMULAIS UN DÉCOLLAGE, UN ATTERRISSAGE, UN VIRAGE SUR L'AILE OU AUTRE !...

MAIS DE LA THÉORIE À LA PRATIQUE, IL Y A UN PAS !... ALORS ACCROCHEZ-VOUS BIEN CAR JE NE VOUS GARANTIS PAS UN ATTERRISSAGE EN DOUCEUR !

AU DÉBUT, JE ME TROMPAIS SOUVENT ET PUIS, PEU À PEU, J'AI PRIS DE L'ASSURANCE !

AVEC UN SANG-FROID INCROYABLE POUR SON ÂGE, IL PARVINT À ATTERRIR SANS DOMMAGE !...

ON AVAIT FRÔLÉ LA CATASTROPHE : SI LE LOURD APPAREIL S'ÉTAIT ÉCRASÉ AU SOL, IL AURAIT FAIT DE NOMBREUSES VICTIMES PARMI LES SPECTATEURS !

À SA DESCENTE D'AVION, IL FUT PORTÉ EN TRIOMPHE PAR LE PUBLIC !... LE LENDEMAIN, SON EXPLOIT FUT RELATÉ PAR LES MÉDIAS LOCAUX ET IL DEVINT UN HÉROS POUR SES COPAINS DE CLASSE QUI LE SURNOMMÈRENT "DAKOTA".

DEPUIS, CE SURNOM LUI EST RESTÉ.

LE VOILÀ !... JE L'APERÇOIS AU LOIN !

DESCENDEZ-LE DANS LA CALE !

JE VIENS DE TÉLÉPHONER À L'ÉTAT-MAJOR : VOTRE MYSTÉRIEUSE DÉCOUVERTE LES INTÉRESSE BOUGREMENT !... ILS M'ONT DONNÉ L'ORDRE DE METTRE IMMÉDIATEMENT LE CAP SUR LA BASE LA PLUS PROCHE OÙ DES SCIENTIFIQUES L'EXAMINERONT. D'ICI LÀ, INTERDICTION FORMELLE D'Y TOUCHER !

À VOS ORDRES, COMMANDANT !

À VOTRE AVIS, DAKOTA, QU'EST-CE QU'IL PEUT BIEN Y AVOIR LÀ-DEDANS ?

JE N'EN AI PAS LA MOINDRE IDÉE !

TOUT CE QUE JE PEUX VOUS DIRE, C'EST QUE CE N'EST PAS RADIOACTIF !... POUR MOI, C'EST L'ESSENTIEL !

VOUS N'ÊTES VRAIMENT PAS CURIEUX !... VOUS N'AVEZ PAS ENVIE DE SAVOIR CE QU'IL CONTIENT ?

J'AI SURTOUT ENVIE D'UNE BONNE DOUCHE BIEN CHAUDE !...

JE MONTE EN PRENDRE UNE DANS MA CABINE. ON REPARLERA DE TOUT ÇA PLUS TARD.

DRÔLE DE TYPE !

POURQUOI DITES-VOUS ÇA ?

PARCE QU'IL A PRIS DES RISQUES ÉNORMES POUR REPÊCHER CE TRUC !... ET TOUT ÇA UNIQUEMENT POUR S'ASSURER QU'IL N'ÉTAIT PAS RADIOACTIF !... C'EST INCROYABLE !

VOUS AVEZ DES ENFANTS, N'EST-CE PAS ?

OUI, COMMANDANT. DEUX GARÇONS.

DAKOTA, LUI, AVAIT UNE PETITE FILLE...

12

PAPY !
PAPY !

REGARDE CE
QUE J'AI TROUVÉ
DANS L'HERBE !...
C'EST QUOI ?

J'EN SAIS RIEN !... LES
GENS JETTENT DES TAS DE
SALOPERIES DANS LA NATURE !...
ILS PRENNENT NOS CHAMPS
POUR DES POUBELLES !

ON CROIRAIT UNE PYRAMIDE,
COMME EN ÉGYPTE !...

JE PEUX L'EMPORTER
POUR JOUER AVEC ?

TA GRAND-MÈRE VA ENCORE
ROUSPÉTER !... TU SAIS BIEN
QU'ELLE VEUT PAS QUE TU
RAMASSES N'IMPORTE QUOI !...
ELLE A TOUJOURS PEUR
QUE TU TE BLESSES ET
QUE ÇA S'INFECTE !

BEN, ON N'A QU'À RIEN LUI
DIRE !... JE LE CACHERAI SOUS
LE HANGAR, COMME ÇA ELLE
LE VERRA PAS !...

CE SERA UN
SECRET ENTRE
NOUS, D'ACCORD ?

15

17

VOUS SAVEZ COMMENT SONT LES GOSSES : CURIEUX ET SANS MÉFIANCE. CET OBJET TROUVÉ DANS L'HERBE ÉTAIT POUR ELLE UN TRÉSOR !... COMMENT AURAIT-ELLE PU SE DOUTER QUE C'ÉTAIT EN FAIT UN MORCEAU DE SATELLITE, EXTRÊMEMENT RADIOACTIF, TOMBÉ DE L'ESPACE ?

ELLE A JOUÉ AVEC PENDANT TOUT LE WEEK-END. C'EST CE QUI L'A TUÉE. ELLE A ÉTÉ TELLEMENT IRRADIÉE QU'ON N'A PAS PU LA SAUVER. ELLE EST MORTE PEU APRÈS. ELLE VENAIT D'AVOIR HUIT ANS.

DAKOTA ADORAIT SA PETITE FILLE. ELLE ÉTAIT LE MIEL DE SA VIE. EN LA PERDANT, IL PERDIT LE GOÛT DE TOUT. MÊME L'ENVIE DE PILOTER...

IL TENTA D'OUBLIER SON CHAGRIN DANS L'IVRESSE : PENDANT DES MOIS, IL DÉRIVA DE BAR EN BAR, NOCTAMBULE INCON-SOLABLE ACCROCHÉ À L'ALCOOL COMME UN NAUFRAGÉ À SA BOUÉE...

UNE NUIT, IVRE MORT, IL S'ENDORMIT SUR LA TOMBE DE SA FILLE. LORSQU'IL ROUVRIT LES YEUX QUELQUES HEURES PLUS TARD, IL APERÇUT UN SATELLITE QUI PASSAIT DANS LE CIEL ÉTOILÉ. IL RESTA LÀ, UN BON MOMENT, À LE REGARDER...

DU FOND DE SON DÉSESPOIR, IL PENSA QUE CE PETIT POINT BRILLANT ÉTAIT UN MESSAGE QUE SA FILLETTE LUI ENVOYAIT DE L'AU-DELÀ...

ET C'EST CETTE NUIT-LÀ QU'IL A DÉCIDÉ DE CRÉER LA BLUE SKY AGENCY, SPÉCIALISÉE DANS LA DESTRUCTION DES SATELLITES HORS D'USAGE QUI MENACENT DE RETOMBER SUR NOTRE PLANÈTE...

IL VIT PRATIQUEMENT TOUTE L'ANNÉE DANS UNE STATION ORBITALE ET NE REDESCEND SUR TERRE QUE DE TEMPS À AUTRE POUR EFFECTUER DES MISSIONS SPÉCIALES...

DEPUIS, IL PASSE LA PLUPART DE SES JOURNÉES À TRAQUER LA FERRAILLE EN ORBITE POUR LA PULVÉRISER. C'EST UN JOB TRÈS DANGEREUX QU'IL EST LE SEUL À OSER FAIRE...

NOTAMMENT POUR DÉTRUIRE LES ÉNORMES ICEBERGS QUI, DEPUIS LA FONTE DES PÔLES, DÉRIVENT DANS L'OCÉAN ARCTIQUE ET REPRÉSENTENT UN TERRIBLE DANGER POUR LE TRAFIC MARITIME.

17

BONJOUR, COMMANDANT !... JE VOUS ATTENDAIS : L'ÉTAT-MAJOR M'A PRÉVENU DE VOTRE ARRIVÉE. ILS M'ONT DIT QUE VOUS AVIEZ FAIT UNE ÉTRANGE DÉCOUVERTE, SANS ME DONNER PLUS DE PRÉCISIONS. DE QUOI S'AGIT-IL EXACTEMENT ?

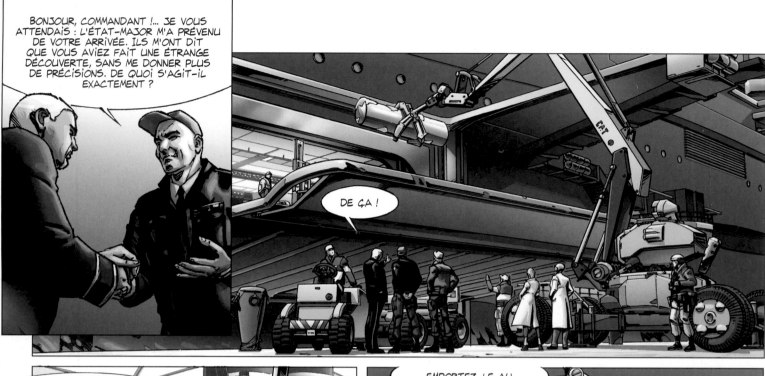

DE ÇA !

JE N'AI JAMAIS RIEN VU DE SEMBLABLE !... ET VOUS, PROFESSEUR ?

NON !

MOI NON PLUS !

EMPORTEZ-LE AU LABORATOIRE !

À VOS ORDRES, AMIRAL.

COMMENT L'AVEZ-VOUS TROUVÉ ?

EN DÉTRUISANT UN ICEBERG !... IL ÉTAIT PRISONNIER DE LA GLACE ET L'EXPLOSION DE LA DERNIÈRE BOMBE L'A PROJETÉ À LA MER.

LA GLACE QUI LE RECOUVRAIT N'A PAS ENTIÈREMENT FONDU PENDANT LE TRAJET, HEUREUSEMENT !... VOUS EN PRÉLÈVEREZ UN ÉCHANTILLON AFIN QUE JE PUISSE L'ANALYSER !

BIEN, PROFESSEUR.

OÙ VOULEZ-VOUS QU'ON LE METTE ?

DANS LA SALLE DE SCANNER !... AVANT DE L'OUVRIR, JE TIENS À M'ASSURER QU'IL NE CONTIENT RIEN DE DANGEREUX !

19

LÀ !...
REGARDEZ !

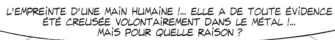

L'EMPREINTE D'UNE MAIN HUMAINE !... ELLE A DE TOUTE ÉVIDENCE ÉTÉ CREUSÉE VOLONTAIREMENT DANS LE MÉTAL !... MAIS POUR QUELLE RAISON ?

VOUS LISEZ TROP DE ROMANS DE SCIENCE-FICTION, NORA !... MAIS, APRÈS TOUT, POURQUOI PAS ?... ON PEUT TOUJOURS ESSAYER !

IL FAUT PEUT-ÊTRE APPUYER DESSUS POUR DÉCLENCHER L'OUVERTURE !

NON, ÇA NE SERT PAS À OUVRIR !... DÉSOLÉ POUR VOUS, MA CHÈRE !

VOUS N'AVEZ PEUT-ÊTRE PAS APPUYÉ ASSEZ FORT !... LAISSEZ-MOI FAIRE !

VOUS AVEZ RAISON, PROFESSEUR : CE N'EST PAS UN MÉCANISME D'OUVERTURE !... IL VA FALLOIR NOUS DÉBROUILLER AUTREMENT !...

MAIS COMMENT ?

CET ALLIAGE NE LAISSE PAS PASSER LES RAYONS X, MAIS IL DOIT ÊTRE POSSIBLE DE LE PERCER !... UN TROU, MÊME DE FAIBLE DIAMÈTRE, SUFFIRAIT À INTRODUIRE UNE CAMÉRA MINIATURISÉE QUI NOUS PERMETTRAIT DE VOIR CE QU'IL Y A À L'INTÉRIEUR !

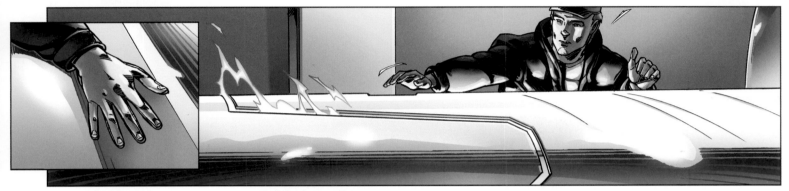

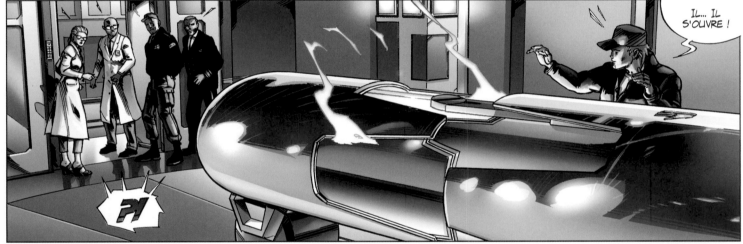

IL... IL S'OUVRE !

FI

COMMENT AVEZ-VOUS FAIT ?!... À QUOI AVEZ-VOUS TOUCHÉ ?

À CETTE EMPREINTE, EXACTEMENT COMME VOUS VENEZ DE LE FAIRE !... ELLE ME RAPPELLE UN DESSIN QUE MA FILLE AVAIT FAIT UN JOUR, À L'ÉCOLE, ALORS J'AI POSÉ LA MAIN DESSUS ET...

OOOOH !

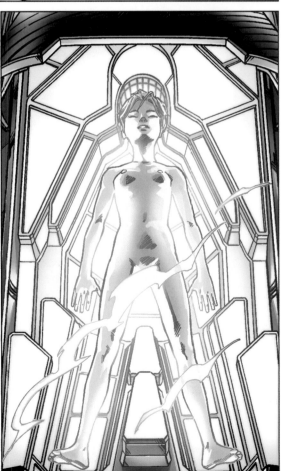

ALORS ?...
QUE VOUS A DIT
LE MINISTRE ?

IL ME RAPPELLERA
DEMAIN !... D'ICI LÀ,
SILENCE ABSOLU SUR CE
DOSSIER QU'IL A D'ORES ET
DÉJÀ DÉCIDÉ DE CLASSER
"SECRET-DÉFENSE" !...
JE COMPTE DONC SUR
VOTRE DISCRÉTION !

J'IGNORE POURQUOI CETTE FILLETTE
EST ENFERMÉE LÀ-DEDANS, MAIS JE
SUIS PERSUADÉ QUE NOUS SOMMES EN
PRÉSENCE D'UNE DES PLUS GRANDES
DÉCOUVERTES ARCHÉOLOGIQUES DU
SIÈCLE !... J'AI HÂTE D'EN SAVOIR
PLUS À SON SUJET ET DE PERCER
LE MYSTÈRE QUI L'ENTOURE !

PATIENCE, PROFESSEUR, VOUS POURREZ TENTER DE RÉSOUDRE
CETTE PASSIONNANTE ÉNIGME SCIENTIFIQUE DÈS QUE J'AURAI
REÇU LE FEU VERT DU MINISTÈRE !

EN ATTENDANT,
INTERDICTION FORMELLE
DE PÉNÉTRER DANS CE
LABORATOIRE SANS MON
AUTORISATION !

PAR MESURE DE SÉCURITÉ, JE
VAIS EN CHANGER IMMÉDIATEMENT
LE CODE D'ACCÈS AFIN D'ÊTRE
LE SEUL À LE CONNAÎTRE.

ET POUR ÉVITER TOUTE TENTATIVE
D'EFFRACTION, UN DE MES HOMMES
RESTERA EN FACTION DEVANT CETTE
PORTE PENDANT TOUTE LA NUIT,
AVEC ORDRE DE NE LAISSER
ENTRER PERSONNE !

AVEZ-VOUS ENCORE BESOIN
DE MOI, COMMANDANT ?

NON, VOTRE MISSION
EST TERMINÉE !...
QU'ALLEZ-VOUS
FAIRE, MAINTENANT ?...
RETOURNER DANS
VOTRE STATION
ORBITALE ?

PAS DIRECTEMENT !... JE VAIS D'ABORD FAIRE
UN CROCHET PAR CHEZ MES PARENTS !...
ÇA FAIT LONGTEMPS QUE JE NE LES AI PAS
VUS ET JE LEUR AI PROMIS DE PASSER
QUELQUES JOURS AVEC EUX.

ILS ONT
TOUJOURS LEUR
EXPLOITATION
AGRICOLE EN
FRANCE ?

OUI !

C'EST POUR ÇA QUE LA SOCIÉTÉ POUR LAQUELLE JE BOSSE A ENGAGÉ DES LASCARS CHARGÉS D'ESCORTER CHAQUE CONVOI !... TU PEUX EN VOIR UN SPÉCIMEN DERRIÈRE MOI...

L'AUTRE SE TROUVE DANS LE WAGON DE QUEUE !

ET POUR PLUS DE SÉCURITÉ, L'HORAIRE ET L'ITINÉRAIRE DES TRAINS NE SONT DÉCIDÉS QU'AU TOUT DERNIER MOMENT !

QUANT À MOI, J'AI POUR CONSIGNE DE FONCER DU DÉPART À L'ARRIVÉE...

ET DE NE M'ARRÊTER SOUS AUCUN PRÉTEXTE EN COURS DE ROUTE...

CHUUT !... ÉCOUTE !

ALLÔ ?... OUI, JE TE REÇOIS CINQ SUR CINQ !... COMMENT ?... UN HÉLICO ?... TU ES SÛR ?

AFFIRMATIF !... IL VIENT TOUT JUSTE D'ÉMERGER DE LA BRUME !... IL SE DIRIGE DROIT SUR NOUS !... TU LE VOIS ?

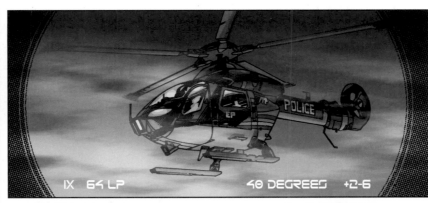

OUI, ÇA Y EST, JE L'APERÇOIS...

IX 64 LP   40 DEGREES   +2-6

SURTOUT PAS, C'EST LA POLICE !

IL SE RAPPROCHE !... QU'EST-CE QUE JE FAIS ?... JE LE DESCENDS ?

IL EST QUATRE HEURES DU MATIN !

ET ALORS ?

LA POLICE À UNE HEURE PAREILLE DANS CE TROU PERDU, TU TROUVES PAS ÇA BIZARRE, TOI ?

BLAW

ARH...

TOM, TU ME REÇOIS ?...
ILS ONT DESCENDU
YVAN !

LES
SALOPARDS !...

BRRAATT

C'EST PAS DES
FLICS, ON S'EST
FAIT AVOIR !

TU LES
AS EUS ?

NON !...
ILS ONT RÉUSSI
À SE BARRER !... ILS
ONT DISPARU DANS
LE BROUILLARD !

BRRATT
RATTBRA

JE N'Y VOIS RIEN AVEC TOUTE CETTE BRUME !... OÙ EST-IL PASSÉ, CE PUTAIN D'HÉLICO ?

BRAAAT!!

AARRH

TOM ?...

TU ME REÇOIS ?... TOM !... QU'EST-CE QUI SE PASSE ?...

RÉPONDS !... TOM !

ARRÊTE LE TRAIN !... OBÉIS OU JE TIRE !

LA FILLE A RÉUSSI À S'ENFUIR !... TU VEUX QUE JE M'EN OCCUPE ?

NON, ON N'A PAS DE TEMPS À PERDRE !... MOINS ON S'ATTARDERA DANS LE SECTEUR, MIEUX ÇA VAUDRA !... GRIMPE DANS LA LOCO ET FONCE !... LES AUTRES T'ATTENDENT AVEC LES CAMIONS POUR RÉCEPTIONNER LA CAMELOTE, JE LES PRÉVIENS QUE TU ARRIVES !

?!

CUI... CUI...

TU VOLES, MAINTENANT ?...
TU AS RAISON : C'EST
MOINS DANGEREUX QUE
DE PRENDRE LE TRAIN !

AH, TE
VOILÀ,
TOI !...

J'AI EU LA TROUILLE, SI TU SAVAIS !...
J'AI BIEN CRU FINIR COMME YVAN ET
TOM... LES PAUVRES... C'ÉTAIENT DE
BRAVES TYPES... JE LES AIMAIS BIEN...

ILS NE
FAISAIENT PAS
CE BOULOT PAR
VOCATION...

... MAIS PARCE
QU'ILS N'AVAIENT
RIEN TROUVÉ
D'AUTRE MALGRÉ
TOUS LEURS
DIPLÔMES.
COMME MOI.

ET ELLE ?... QUI C'EST, À
TON AVIS ?... QU'EST-CE
QU'ELLE FICHAIT LÀ, NUE
COMME UN VER EN TRAVERS
DE LA VOIE ?... SANS DOUTE
ENCORE UNE GAMINE
VICTIME D'UN CRIME
DE SADIQUE !

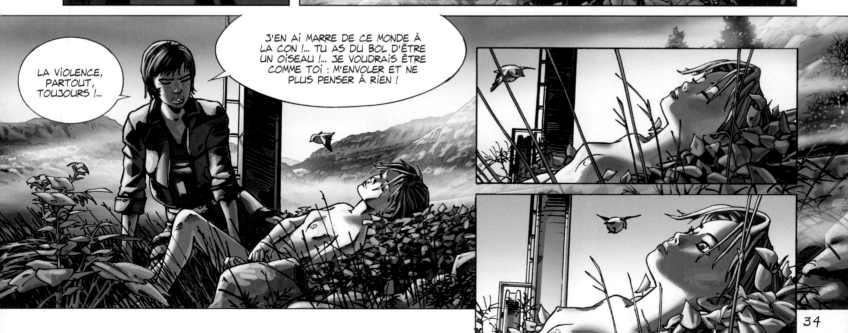
LA VIOLENCE,
PARTOUT,
TOUJOURS !...

J'EN AI MARRE DE CE MONDE À
LA CON !... TU AS DU BOL D'ÊTRE
UN OISEAU !... JE VOUDRAIS ÊTRE
COMME TOI : M'ENVOLER ET NE
PLUS PENSER À RIEN !

ALLÔ ?...

AH, C'EST VOUS, COMMANDANT !... NON, NON, VOUS NE ME DÉRANGEZ PAS : JE SUIS EN TRAIN D'AIDER MON PÈRE À ENSEMENCER SES CHAMPS !

COMMENT VA-T-IL DEPUIS LA DERNIÈRE FOIS QUE JE L'AI VU ?... EST-IL TOUJOURS FAROUCHEMENT OPPOSÉ AUX OGM ?

PLUS QUE JAMAIS !... C'EST UN FERVENT DÉFENSEUR DE L'AGRICULTURE NATURELLE ET BIOLOGIQUE. EN BON ÉCOLO QU'IL EST, IL N'UTILISE NI ENGRAIS CHIMIQUES NI PESTICIDES.

MAIS J'IMAGINE, COMMANDANT, QUE CE N'EST PAS POUR DÉBATTRE DE QUESTIONS AGRICOLES QUE VOUS ME TÉLÉPHONEZ !... ALORS, POURQUOI ?

36

38

PARCE QUE NOUS AVONS UN PROBLÈME, DAKOTA !... UN TRÈS GROS PROBLÈME : LA FILLETTE A DISPARU !

JE NE PEUX PAS VOUS EN DIRE PLUS AU TÉLÉPHONE.

JE VOUS EXPLIQUERAI TOUT ÇA EN DÉTAIL DE VIVE VOIX.

C'EST TRÈS IMPORTANT !

L'AMIRAL, LE PROFESSEUR ET MOI-MÊME AVONS RENDEZ-VOUS EN DÉBUT D'APRÈS-MIDI AVEC LE MINISTRE EUROPÉEN DE LA DÉFENSE. VOTRE PRÉSENCE NOUS SEMBLE À TOUS INDISPENSABLE !... POUVEZ-VOUS VENIR ?...

OK, J'Y SERAI. VOUS POUVEZ COMPTER SUR MOI.

C'ÉTAIT LE COMMANDANT BRICK. IL ME DEMANDE DE LE REJOINDRE AU MINISTÈRE.

TA MÈRE VA ÊTRE DÉÇUE, ELLE QUI ESPÉRAIT QUE TU RESTERAIS DÉJEUNER AVEC NOUS !... COMMENT TU VAS ALLER LÀ-BAS ?... EN VOITURE ?

NON !...

AVEC LES LIMITATIONS DE VITESSE ET LES EMBOUTEILLAGES, JE RISQUE D'ARRIVER EN RETARD. J'IRAI PLUS VITE EN PARAMOTOR !... ILS EN LOUENT À L'AÉRODROME, TU SAIS, CELUI OÙ J'ALLAIS QUAND J'ÉTAIS GOSSE.

TU PEUX M'Y CONDUIRE ?

BIEN SÛR !

37

... ET C'EST EN M'ENFUYANT DANS LE TUNNEL QUE J'AI BUTÉ SUR CETTE FILLETTE. ELLE ÉTAIT ÉTENDUE EN TRAVERS DE LA VOIE, COMPLÈTEMENT NUE.

PAUVRE GOSSE, ELLE A CERTAINEMENT ÉTÉ ENLEVÉE PAR UN SADIQUE !

OUI, MAIS POUR ÇA, IL FAUT QUE TU ME DONNES LEUR NUMÉRO DE TÉLÉPHONE !... TU LE CONNAIS ?

ÇA M'ÉTONNERAIT QU'ELLE VOUS RÉPONDE : ELLE N'A PAS PRONONCÉ LE MOINDRE MOT DEPUIS QUE JE L'AI TROUVÉE !... À MON AVIS, ELLE N'EST PAS FRANÇAISE.

DANS CE CAS, ON VA PROCÉDER DIFFÉREMMENT !

C'EST CE QUE J'AI PENSÉ !... ALORS JE VOUS L'AI AMENÉE POUR QUE VOUS PUISSIEZ PRÉVENIR SES PARENTS.

ANNA, S'IL VOUS PLAÎT, CONTACTEZ TOUTES LES UNITÉS DE GENDARMERIE DE MÉTROPOLE. DEMANDEZ-LEUR SI, PAR HASARD, ILS N'AURAIENT PAS REÇU UN AVIS DE DISPARITION CORRESPONDANT AU SIGNALEMENT DE CETTE PETITE.

BIEN SÛR !... MAIS LE TGV NE S'ARRÊTE PLUS ICI. DEPUIS LA PRIVATISATION, ILS ONT FERMÉ LA GARE. PAS ASSEZ RENTABLE, PARAÎT-IL !... ALORS IL VOUS FAUDRA PRENDRE L'AUTOCAR. IL EN PASSE UN TOUS LES APRÈS-MIDI.

D'ACCORD, JE LEUR ENVOIE UN MAIL IMMÉDIATEMENT !

BON, PENDANT CE TEMPS-LÀ, JE VAIS PRENDRE VOTRE DÉPOSITION DÉTAILLÉE SUR LES CIRCONSTANCES QUI ONT COÛTÉ LA VIE À VOS DEUX COLLÈGUES.

APRÈS, JE POURRAI RENTRER CHEZ MOI ?

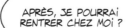

COMME JE VOUS L'AI DIT TOUT À L'HEURE AU TÉLÉPHONE, DAKOTA, LA FILLETTE A DISPARU !... C'EST EN ENTRANT CE MATIN DANS LE LABORATOIRE QUE L'AMIRAL S'EST APERÇU QU'ELLE N'ÉTAIT PLUS LÀ !

LE COMMANDANT, LE PROFESSEUR, SON ASSISTANTE ET MOI-MÊME L'AVONS CHERCHÉE PARTOUT !... EN VAIN !... NOUS NE L'AVONS PAS RETROUVÉE !

QU'EST-ELLE DEVENUE ?... NOUS L'IGNORONS !... TOUT CE QUE NOUS POUVONS AFFIRMER, C'EST QU'ELLE N'EST PLUS DANS LA BASE !

ET LE GARDE QUE VOUS AVIEZ POSTÉ ?... VOUS L'AVEZ INTERROGÉ ?

IL A ÉTÉ TUÉ. JE L'AI TROUVÉ MORT DANS LE COULOIR, DEVANT LA PORTE, EN ARRIVANT AU LABO. D'APRÈS LE MÉDECIN LÉGISTE, IL A ÉTÉ ASSASSINÉ VERS MINUIT.

RESTE À SAVOIR PAR QUI !... AVEZ-VOUS DÉCOUVERT UN INDICE QUELCONQUE QUI PUISSE FAIRE AVANCER VOTRE ENQUÊTE ?

HÉLAS NON, MONSIEUR LE MINISTRE !... PAS LA MOINDRE PISTE !... ET AUCUN TÉMOIN !

BIZARRE QUE PERSONNE N'AIT RIEN VU NI RIEN ENTENDU !

CELA S'EXPLIQUE PAR LA CONFIGURATION DES LIEUX. LE COULOIR DONT PARLAIT L'AMIRAL MÈNE UNIQUEMENT À MON LABORATOIRE. LA NUIT, IL EST TOTALEMENT DÉSERT. PERSONNE N'Y PASSE. C'EST POURQUOI LE OU LES MEURTRIERS ONT PU AGIR SANS ATTIRER L'ATTENTION.

À MON AVIS, ILS ONT ASSASSINÉ LE GARDE, PUIS FORCÉ LE SYSTÈME D'OUVERTURE DE LA PORTE ET ENLEVÉ LA FILLETTE.

À MOINS QUE CE NE SOIT L'INVERSE !... C'EST PEUT-ÊTRE LA FILLETTE QUI A FORCÉ CE SYSTÈME AVANT DE TUER LE GARDE POUR S'ENFUIR !

C'EST COMPLÈTEMENT IMPOSSIBLE !... EN ADMETTANT MÊME QU'ELLE SOIT SUBITEMENT SORTIE DE L'ÉTAT LÉTHARGIQUE DANS LEQUEL ELLE ÉTAIT PLONGÉE, COMMENT VOULEZ-VOUS QUE CETTE GAMINE AIT PU NEUTRALISER À ELLE SEULE UN TYPE ARMÉ ET ENTRAÎNÉ AU COMBAT !

CETTE "GAMINE", COMME VOUS DITES, A 10 000 ANS !

QUOI ?!... VOUS PLAISANTEZ ?

PAS DU TOUT !... J'AI PU DÉTERMINER SON ÂGE EN ANALYSANT LES ÉCHANTILLONS DE GLACE QUE NOUS AVONS PRÉLEVÉS SUR LE CAISSON.

C'EST UNE INDICATION IMPORTANTE, PROFESSEUR STINGER, MAIS CELA NE NOUS DIT PAS POURQUOI ELLE ÉTAIT ENFERMÉE DANS CE CAISSON, NI D'OÙ ELLE VIENT !... POUR TENTER DE PERCER CE MYSTÈRE, IL FAUT LA RETROUVER...

ET POUR ÇA, MON CHER DAKOTA, JE COMPTE SUR VOUS !

SUR MOI ?!... POURQUOI ?

PARCE QUE VOUS AVEZ VU SON VISAGE. VOUS POURREZ DONC LA RECONNAÎTRE.

JE NE SUIS PAS LE SEUL : LE COMMANDANT, L'AMIRAL, LE PROFESSEUR ET SON ASSISTANTE L'ONT VU ÉGALEMENT !

40

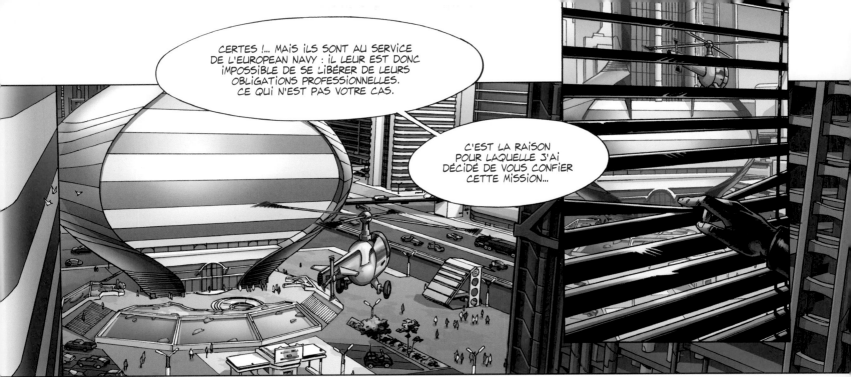

CERTES !... MAIS ILS SONT AU SERVICE DE L'EUROPEAN NAVY : IL LEUR EST DONC IMPOSSIBLE DE SE LIBÉRER DE LEURS OBLIGATIONS PROFESSIONNELLES. CE QUI N'EST PAS VOTRE CAS.

C'EST LA RAISON POUR LAQUELLE J'AI DÉCIDÉ DE VOUS CONFIER CETTE MISSION...

... IL VA DE SOI QUE VOUS SEREZ RÉMUNÉRÉ EN CONSÉQUENCE. VOTRE PRIX SERA LE MIEN. EN CONTREPARTIE, MON CHER DAKOTA, J'ATTENDS DE VOUS DES RÉSULTATS RAPIDES. JE VOUS LAISSE CARTE BLANCHE POUR MENER VOTRE ENQUÊTE...

... JE VOUS DEMANDE SEULEMENT D'AGIR AVEC LA PLUS GRANDE DISCRÉTION, CAR SI CERTAINS PAYS ÉTRANGERS APPRENAIENT L'EXISTENCE DE CETTE "CRÉATURE", ILS TENTERAIENT À COUP SÛR DE S'EN EMPARER !...

... CE DOSSIER DOIT DONC RESTER CONFIDENTIEL !... C'EST POUR ÇA QUE JE L'AI CLASSÉ "SECRET-DÉFENSE" ET QUE JE LUI AI DONNÉ UN NOM DE CODE : ARCTICA !

ÇA Y EST, LEUR PETITE RÉUNION EST TERMINÉE !

TU AS RÉUSSI À TOUT ENREGISTRER ?

OUI !

41

NON !... LES GENDARMERIES AUXQUELLES J'AI ENVOYÉ LE MAIL M'ONT TOUTES RÉPONDU PAR LA NÉGATIVE : ON NE LEUR A SIGNALÉ AUCUNE DISPARITION D'ENFANT DE CET ÂGE.

TOUJOURS RIEN DE NEUF AU SUJET DE LA GAMINE ?

BON, EH BIEN ON VA DE NOUVEAU L'INTERROGER !... ON NE SAIT JAMAIS : À FORCE DE PATIENCE, ON FINIRA PEUT-ÊTRE PAR DÉCOUVRIR QUELLE LANGUE ELLE PARLE !

ON PEUT TOUJOURS ESSAYER !... JE VAIS LA CHERCHER !

ELLE... ELLE N'EST PLUS LÀ !... ELLE S'EST ENFUIE PAR LA FENÊTRE !

PAR LA FENÊTRE ?!... C'EST IMPOSSIBLE, VOYONS, IL Y A DES BARREAUX !

ELLE LES A SCIÉS !

QUOI ?!

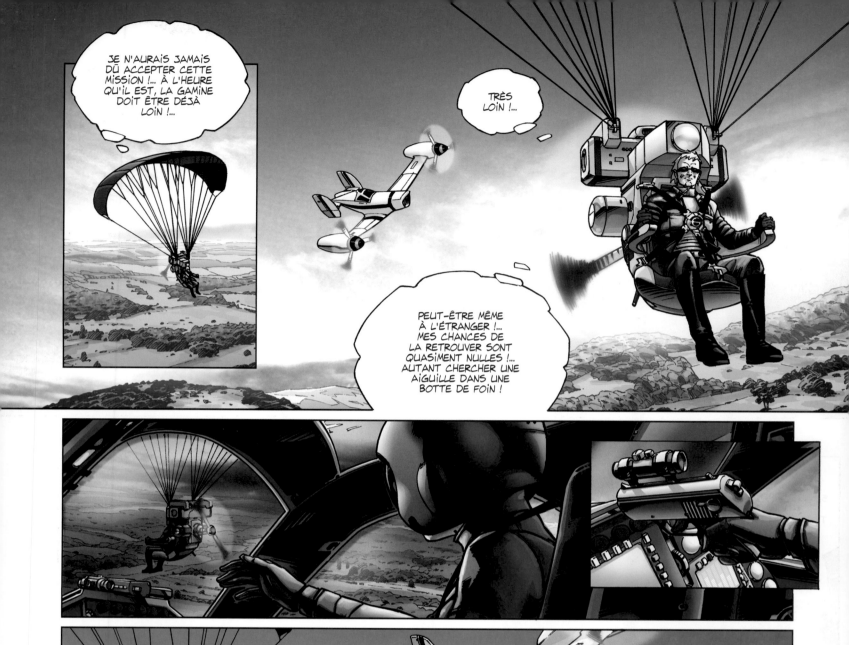

44

POURQUOI CE CINGLÉ M'A-T-IL TIRÉ DESSUS ?!... EN TOUT CAS, IL A VISIBLEMENT L'INTENTION DE RECOMMENCER CAR IL FAIT DEMI-TOUR !

IMPOSSIBLE DE LE SEMER, JE SUIS PLUS LENT QUE LUI, SURTOUT AVEC MES SUSPENTES ENDOMMAGÉES !... ET SI JE ME POSE, CE SERA ENCORE PIRE : JE FERAI UNE CIBLE EN OR, IL NE POURRA PAS ME LOUPER !... C'EST FOUTU, JE N'AI AUCUNE CHANCE DE LUI ÉCHAPPER !

À MOINS QUE... OUI, IL Y A PEUT-ÊTRE UNE SOLUTION !... MAIS IL VA FALLOIR AGIR VITE !... TRÈS VITE !... ET JOUER SUR L'EFFET DE SURPRISE !

BON, ALLONS-Y !...

D'ABORD RALENTIR POUR QU'IL ME RATTRAPE JUSTE AVANT DE SURVOLER L'ÉTANG... PUIS ATTENDRE QU'IL SOIT À LA BONNE DISTANCE...

APPROCHE, SALOPARD... ENCORE...

ENCORE UN PEU...

MAINTENANT !

KLIK !

45

Electrocution   There are many other factors besides hunting that affect migrating birds, and one of them is electrocution on high-tension electrical wires. Migrating birds stopping to rest on electrical poles are often electrocuted. When large soaring birds, such as storks, simultaneously touch two high tension wires with their outspread wings, or when they stand on one arm of a high-voltage pole and touch a wire above it with their heads, they are electrocuted. Electrical poles attract migrating birds as a convenient and safe site for roosting, particularly in open desert areas where there are no trees. In Israel a number of storks were electrocuted in the spring on the high-tension wires in an area north of Beersheba. A major stork spring migration axis overlies this region, used by storks flying from Africa to their breeding quarters in northern Europe. Flocks of migrating storks sometimes land as evening approaches, to roost on the high power electrical poles. Electrocuted individuals sometimes fall to the ground, but in cases where one remains on the pole overnight, it short-circuits the system and causes electrical failures in adjacent settlements and industrial plants. The Israel Electric Company has built special devices for all high-tension electrical poles in the area, to prevent storks landing on dangerous parts of the pole. This solution has guarded against further harm to the migrating storks and stopped the electrical failures in the area as well.

In 1996 the Israel Electric Company joined the Israel Nature Reserves Authority and the Society for the Protection of Nature in Israel in a project named "Spreading Wings over Griffon Vultures". The major goal of this project is to prevent the extinction of this species in Israel. Large-scale solutions for bird electrocutions are being implemented as part of this project, including the use of specially designed protective devices to prevent the electrocution of migratory species such as White Storks and Pelicans. Ofer Bahat, co-author of this book, coordinates this project.

Pesticides   Another factor affecting migrating birds, particularly in their winter quarters, is the use of non-degradable pesticides in agriculture. These cause secondary poisoning of raptors and sometimes of other birds such as storks and owls as well. In the past, destructive pesticides such as Azodrin were widely used in Israel against rodents. The raptors preying on them were in turn affected by the chemicals that had accumulated in the rodent bodies and were poisoned in masses. In the Hula Valley each winter for many years, dozens of raptors were poisoned and died, including rare species such as the White-tailed Eagle and the Imperial Eagle. For the last decade the use of pesticides has been illegal in Israel. In other parts of the world too, migrating birds have been severely hurt by pesticides. The Peregrine population that bred in the arctic areas of North America was badly hurt by pesticide contamination in their winter quarters in Central and South America. European and Asian raptor populations suffered secondary poisoning in Africa due to pesticide use.

In most developed countries use of non-degradable pesticides is now banned and any use of pesticides is stringently regulated. Unfortunately there are many loopholes in the enforcement of these regulations and in reality migrating birds are still exposed to great danger, as is the entire natural environment, from the use of pesticides.

Damage to natural areas   Destruction of natural habitats as a result of human activity is another factor significantly affecting the survival of migrating birds. During the past decades tremendous expansion for construction, agriculture and industry has been taking place in developing countries. One well-known case of environmental development In Israel that had a significant effect on migrating birds, was the drainage of the Hula Lake in 1954. Before the drainage, the Hula Lake was a haven for hundreds of thousands of wintering and resting birds on their way from Europe and Asia to Africa and back. After the drainage only the Hula Nature Reserve, a small remnant of the original lake, was left. As a result the area suitable for wintering waterfowl was severely reduced, although the development of agriculture in the drained lands brought new species, such as the Crane, that had not wintered before in the area. Massive construction and transformation of open spaces into settlements or industrial areas causes constant shrinkage of potential feeding and resting sites for passage migrants and wintering birds. Accelerated development in Israel is constantly reducing available feeding and resting sites for migrating birds, with a resultant decrease in their total numbers. In order to protect migrating birds, conservation organizations in various parts of the world are investing efforts to prevent habitat destruction, hunting and other harmful factors that can lead to the extinction of rare species and endanger others.

Page 106:
An F-15 fighter plane in a flock of storks.
(Drawing: James P. Smith)

Electrical Company workers taking down an electrocuted White Stork from a high-tension power pole north of Beersheba.
(Photo: Yossi Leshem)

A pile of dead Black Kites poisoned in the Hula Valley.
(Photo: Yossi Va'adiya)

Pages 104-105:
An F-16 fighter plane flying over the southern Dead Sea.
(Photo: Duby Tal, Albatross Inc.)

103

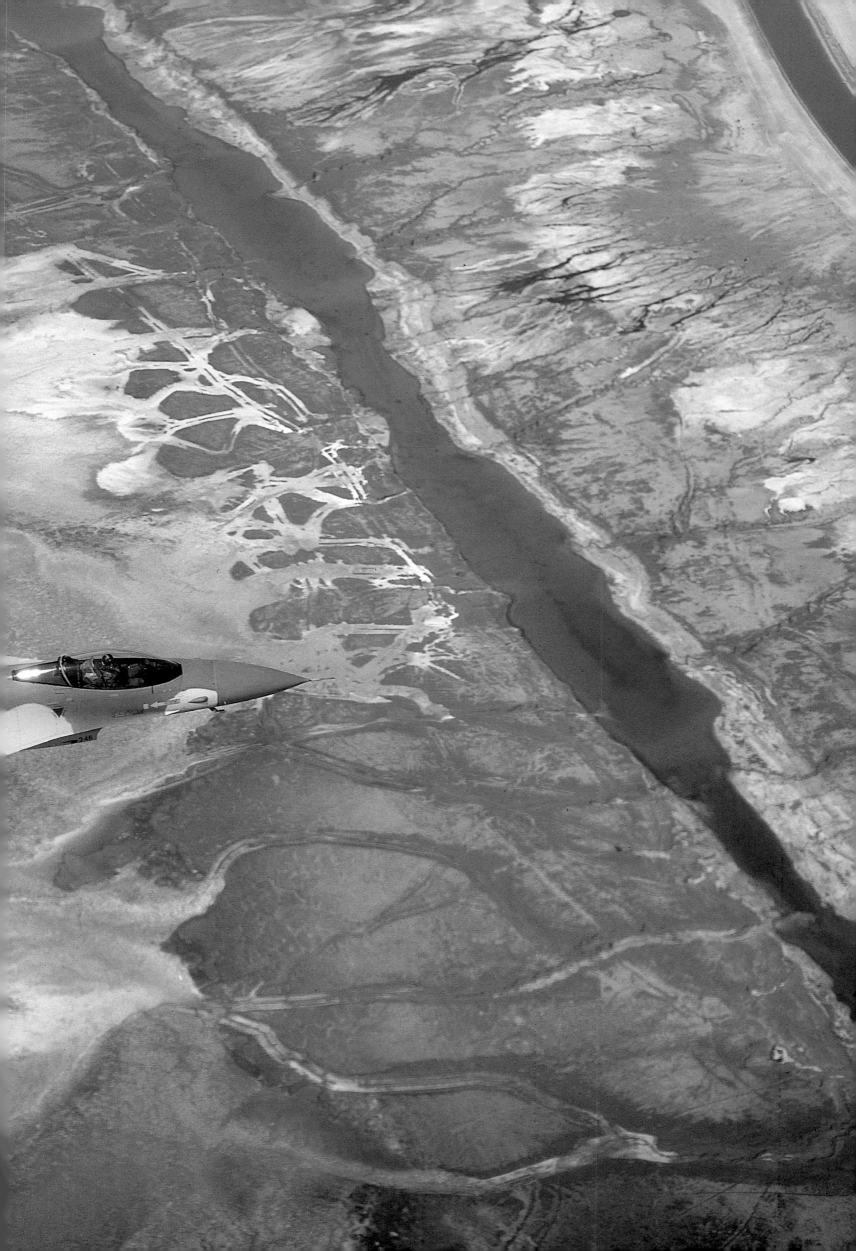

Chapter 3

Aircraft and Birds - Conflict or Coexistence?

אִם־תַּגְבִּיהַּ כַּנֶּשֶׁר וְאִם־בֵּין כּוֹכָבִים שִׂים קִנֶּךָ (עובדיה א׳, ד)

"Though thou make thy nest as high as the vulture..."
(Obadiah, 1:4)

Page 108:
F-15 Eagle of the Israel Air Force flying
above the desert.
(Photo: Israel Air Force)

A. *The Vast Damages Suffered by the Israel Air Force from Migrating Birds*

In 1977, Ehud Dovrat, one of Israel's leading birdwatchers, discovered an unknown raptor migration route in the Kfar Qasem area in central Israel, on the western slopes of the Samarian mountains. By 1980 The Society for the Protection of Nature in Israel's Raptor Information Center had started organizing surveys to count the migrating birds flying over the area. Interest in bird migration in Israel has grown over the years and more than 150 birdwatchers have participated in migration counts across the country during autumn migration along the cross-Samaria highway, from the Greater Tel-Aviv area to the Jordan Valley.

Data from these surveys showed that there is massive soaring bird migration over Israel, mainly birds of prey, storks and pelicans, in numbers greater than those known till then from other parts of the world. In time it became clear that the information was incomplete, since the surveys were based on data from ground observations at fixed sites. In winter of 1983, Yossi Leshem and Ehud Dovrat proposed establishing a joint program to the Israel Air Force (IAF). Data gathered by ground-based observers up to that point would be passed on to the air force in order to warn them about possible collisions with migrating birds. In return, the IAF would help SPNI birdwatchers locate principal migration routes and their altitudes by contributing light aircraft flight hours to complement the data gathered from the ground.

The canopy of a Bell-212 helicopter (named "heron" in the IAF) shattered by a Black-headed Gull. The gull crashed through the canopy, injured the pilot's face and was followed by another gull that wounded the pilot's neck.
(Photo: Yossi Leshem)

From early contacts with IAF officers they learned, to their surprise, that the magnitude of the conflict between our planes and migrating birds was far beyond what they had imagined (numbers were classified at the time). Birds hit fighter aircraft every year and the financial cost was enormous.

The convergence of large numbers of soaring birds, sometimes in waves of tens or even hundreds of thousands daily, into Israel's limited air space, created a serious flight safety problem for the air force planes and their pilots. The problem became even more severe after the Sinai Peninsula was returned to Egypt in April 1982. Sinai had been the major training ground for the IAF and after its return significantly reduced the available air space for training flights and military maneuvers.

Analysis of the data on aircraft-bird collisions in the Israel Air Force between 1972-1982 showed that hundreds of cases of birdstrike had occurred. Most of the collisions occurred during the major migration months in spring (March, April and May) and in autumn (September and October). Three-quarters of the most serious air collisions, in which the aircraft crashed or damage exceeded one-half million

Total number of serious fighter aircraft collisions in the Israel Air Force for the period between 1972 and 1982

Aircraft type	Mirage 5	F-15 - Eagle	F-4 - Phantom	Kfir	A-4 - Skyhawk	Total
Damage 3 (serious)	1	2	4	3	15	25
Damage 4 (very serious)	-	1	-	1	2	4
Damage 5 (total loss)	1	-	-	1	2	4
Total	2	3	4	5	19	33

The total number of birdstrikes on a monthly scale between 1972 and 1996 in the Israel Air Force fighter plane fleet. Most of the collisions took place during spring migration in March, April and May and during autumn migration in September and October.

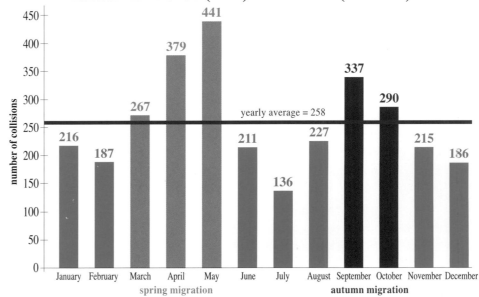

Twenty five years of air collisions with birds in the Israel Air Force (IAF) 1972-1996 (N=3092)

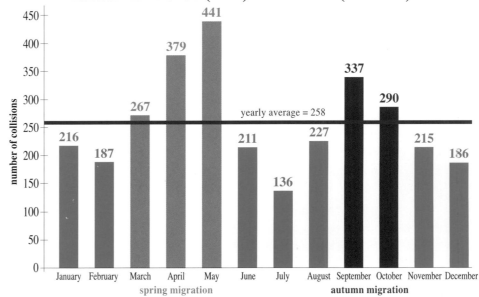

A Black Kite colliding with a fighter plane flying at 800 k.p.h., hits it with a force of 22.7 tons.
(Photo: Ofer Bahat)

dollars, took place during migration months due to migrating birds. During this decade the air force suffered damages exceeding tens of millions of dollars and in October 1974 pilot Major Sephi Levine was killed in a collision with a migrating pelican over the Hula Valley.

In addition to the serious collisions there were another 254 less severe ones (damage magnitude 1-2). Most of the serious collisions took place with fighter planes. The force of the hit is directly related to the flight speed of the aircraft and the bird, and to their weight: the faster a plane flies and the heavier the bird striking it, the stronger the hit and the greater the damage.

The force with which different birds strike aircraft

Species	Bird mass (grams)	Relative speed of collision (k.p.h.)	Force of collision with the aircraft (tons)
Hooded Crow	450	800	15.1
Black Kite	900	800	22.7
Griffon Vulture	6,000	800	40.0
White Pelican	9,500	800	100.0

Birdstrike is an international problem, but in Israel, with its unique geographic location, it is particularly serious. The Israel Air Force maneuvers in limited air space filled with hundreds of millions of migrating birds for 7 months every year, so collisions are nearly inevitable with serious financial damage, not to mention the danger to pilot lives.

In winter of 1983 Yossi Leshem and Ehud Dovrat proposed to the IAF Command that a Cessna be used to track migrating birds to locate flock routes and assess the magnitude of migration. When the extent of the damage migrating birds cause to the Israel Air Force became evident, Yossi Leshem suggested developing a joint research project, as part of a Ph. D. thesis, with the IAF, the SPNI, Tel-Aviv University and the Ministry of Science. The purpose of the project was to analyze soaring bird migration routes over Israel, migration timing, altitude and numbers. The results were to be applied immediately in the air force training program, with the aim of drastically reducing the probability of bird-aircraft collisions. Soaring birds (pelicans, storks and birds of prey) that are large, heavy birds became the focus of the study since they cause most of the serious damage to the IAF.

110

While the subject was being discussed another severe collision occurred, leading to a decision to commence research immediately. During the first week of May, the peak of Honey Buzzard spring migration, when three-quarters of a million Honey Buzzards fly over Israel, one of them hit a Skyhawk fighter plane. The collision took place on 5 May 1983 when the Skyhawk was flying at an altitude of 300 feet and a speed of 420 knots (about 765 kilometers per hour!) west of Hebron. The Honey Buzzard struck the canopy, shattered it, entered the cockpit and hit the pilot seat ejection handle. First Lieutenant Y shot out of the plane and fractured a vertebra in his neck, parachuted unconscious to the ground and was miraculously saved, while his craft continued flying uncontrolled for another 50 kilometers until it crashed. Once again a fighter aircraft worth millions of dollars was destroyed and a pilot badly injured as result of birdstrike. Following this severe collision Major General Amos Lapidot, then commander of the air force, immediately approved the joint IAF, SPNI and Tel-Aviv University research project, in order to find solutions for the problem.

B. From the Fighter Pilots' Mouths - a Series of Severe Collisions with Birds

A Golden Eagle in flight.
(Photo: Ofer Bahat)

Collisions with birds pose a severe threat to pilot lives and aircraft endurance. The danger is greatest for fighter aircraft that fly at great speeds, when the time period between the moment the pilot sees and identifies a flock of birds and time is so short, that it is usually impossible for either side to react in time and avoid the collision.

Several cases, of hundreds recorded in the Israel Air Force (IAF) during the past two decades, illustrate the inability of pilots to prevent air collisions with birds, the serious danger the birds pose, and the damage caused by birdstrike.

The eagle that downed a "hawk"   In December 1988, on a stormy, rainy day, Lieutenant R took off on a training flight in his F-16 fighter aircraft, called a "hawk" in the IAF, second in the flight formation. The planes flew over the Judean Desert at a speed of 800 kilometers per hour and an altitude of 200 meters above ground level. Lieutenant R suddenly noticed a large black mass flying towards his plane's canopy. "At first I didn't understand what was happening. Afterwards I realized it was a bird. Only later did I learn that it was a Golden Eagle (a large raptor, resident year round in the desert areas of Israel). I was certain that collision was unavoidable, either I would hit it, or it would hit me. At the last second the bird deflected to my left, towards the wing and the crash was avoided. I shuddered and had a premonition that I was in for it. All of a sudden I saw a second bird exactly like the first. I thought to myself - that's it, I am done for. But instead of shattering the canopy, the bird passed under me towards the engine. When you are in the cockpit you don't hear a thing. You sit protected in your bubble and listen to the immense silence around. Suddenly there was a loud blast. The engine gave its last cry - an awful screech and made stalling sounds. I knew it was shot and that I had to do two things immediately: climb, pulling the stick in order to move away from the ground, and report over the radio to the others in the formation what had happened. In an instant I realized I couldn't even do this. One of the damaged engine blades hit the gas and oil tanks, penetrated the plane's body, making the nose point upwards. The plane started spinning. In case like these there is no choice but to bail out. I had to activate the ejection seat by pulling the handle between my legs, supposedly a simple task, but I couldn't. I blacked-out and when that happens you fly with your eyes open but don't see a thing. When the plane nose points up in a stall like this one, it means doing a G17 maneuver, which means the pull of gravity on the plane and what is in it is 17 times normal. In this situation, it is as if a man weighing 70 kilograms multiplies his weight by 17, to 1,200 kilograms. Muscles can't deal with such a situation. Blood doesn't reach the eyes and brain and you lose consciousness. I tried desperately to bring my hands to the ejection handle and pull, but I couldn't find it because my sight was gone and I couldn't raise my arms because of the weight,

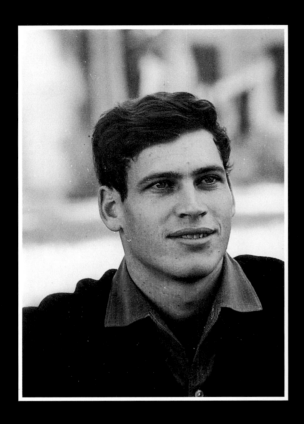

A fateful accident with a pelican Major Sephi Levine from Kibbutz Ma'agan Mikhael was born on 3 February 1947. He became one of the first Skyhawk pilots in the Israel Air Force and knew his aircraft perfectly, the ideal combination of a pilot and a systems man. In the Yom Kippur War (1973) he fought mainly on the southern front but also on the Syrian front. During his first flight in the war his Skyhawk was hit by enemy fire and started burning in the air. The pilot flying alongside him told him to bailout, but he answered that as long as the plane could fly, he wasn't bailing out. In the end he managed to land his flaming plane safely.

After the war Major Sephi Levine was made commander of a Skyhawk fighter squadron.

On 28 October 1974, at the height of pelican migration, while on attack maneuvers in northern Israel, Major Levine was leading a Skyhawk formation at low altitude. At 12:56, in the area of Yesod Hama'alah in the Hula Valley, while he was directing the attack formation, a pelican struck his aircraft. The canopy shattered, Major Levine suffered a direct hit and was killed instantly.

The inquiry following the crash showed beyond any doubt that birdstrike was the cause of the pilot's death and the plane's crash. Following these conclusions the IAF issued strict instructions that closed the Hula Valley to low-altitude flights. In addition, stringent safety instructions on the subject of birdstrike were included in all commands for training and operational flights in the Israel Air Force.

A Skyhawk fighter plane (called an "eagle" in the Israel Air Force) on a low-altitude flight over the Judean Desert.
(Photo: Gil Arbel, Israel Air Force Magazine)

The pilot, Captain Ronen Lev
18.6.1971-10.8.1995

The navigator, Captain Yaron Vivente
29.11.1973-10.8.1995

The Stork that bent a "falcon" wing   August 10, 1995 was a typical sunny summer day at the "falcon" (the nickname for F-15 fighter planes) squadron base, somewhere in central Israel. The pilot, Captain Ronen Lev (24) and his navigator, Captain Yaron Vivente (22), boarded their aircraft and closed the canopy, off on an exhausting training flight in the Negev skies. Captain Lev was born in Haifa, and had been the distinguished graduate of his flight-training course. Captain Vivente, from Giv'at Olga, had been an outstanding student during his four years at the Haifa Military Academy.

At exactly 9:43 A.M., the aircraft were flying in formation at a low altitude of about 1000 feet and at a high speed of 540 knots (about 1000 kilometers per hour), led by the squadron commander Lt. Colonel Sh. He suddenly saw a long train of fire from the left engine of plane number 3 in the formation. The squadron commander reacted unbelievably fast, and managed to shout three times into the radio: "Eject number 3". But for Ronen and Yaron it was too late. Their plane hit the ground in the Nahal Tsin wadi bed, and its parts flew all over. Two of our best fighters had lost their lives.

Preliminary checks by the other pilots showed no reason for the crash - no bird flocks had been seen in the area and there had been no report of any technical problem. The rescue helicopters arrived rapidly at the site and the accident investigation team started surveying the area. They soon found the reason for the terrible tragedy: the remains of two storks that had hit the defunct F-15. In a close examination of the left engine remains of a third stork that had entered the air vent were found, and this was the bird considered actually responsible for the crash. A stork weighing about three kilograms enters an engine extremely rapidly with a force that can reach forty tons. The stork shred the engine blades that scattered and hit the steering mechanism. Within 5 seconds the plane crashed, and the pilot and navigator were tragically unable to eject.

Fate cruelly brought about this unfortunate meeting between three storks and a fighter plane and caused two precious lives to be lost. The collision occurred in one of the BPZs in the Negev, exactly 5 days before BPZ regulations go into effect, during the season the large stork flocks fly over the area.

Two months before the fatal accident, the pilot, Captain Ronen Lev, flew his F-15 plane
(the lowest in the flight formation) during the celebrations of Israel's independence day.

Remains of the F-15 scattered in an area of 400x400 meters in Nahal Zin.

Remains of the two storks that collided with the F-15.
(Photos: Rubi Kastro)

A drawing by the pilot, Captain Ronen Lev, at the age of 5: a flight formation with a bird touching the left wing of one of the planes, seems a premonition of the accident 19 years later, when a stork flew into his left engine.

The remains of navigator Captain Yaron Vivente's watch whose hands stopped at 9:43 from the force of the collision.

A migrating Honey Buzzard. Several fighter planes were hit as a result of collisions with Honey Buzzards.
(Photo: Paul Doherty)

An F-16 fighter plane flying above the clouds.
(upper photo: Gil Arbel, Israel Air Force Magazine)

Remains of an F-16 tail hit by a Golden Eagle over the Judean Desert in December 1988.
(lower photo: courtesy of the Israel Air Force)

which paralyzed me completely. It is a terrible feeling of total loss of control over your body. I was on the verge of fainting but knew I couldn't afford to lose consciousness. At one point I managed to recover, saw the ejection handle, but couldn't drag my hand to it. But I guess when you are faced with death, the body does everything to survive. I don't know where I got the strength, but I suddenly managed to move one hand to the ejection handle and wrenched it". Lieutenant R bailed out of his aircraft on his back in a dive. Luckily the ejection seat is activated by rocket power and it raised him so he could parachute. The strong winds (35 knots) dragged him with his parachute for hundreds of meters over rocky ground and his entire body was bruised from the strong blows he suffered. As a result of the collision with a lone Golden Eagle Lieutenant R's life was saved only by a miracle, and the Israel Air Force lost an F-16 fighter plane, worth close to 27 million dollars!!

The maiden flight of the "Sa'ar" almost ended in disaster

Lt. Colonel (res.) Yohanan Roser is one of the most experienced test pilots in the Israel Air Force. In 1970 he was flying a Sa'ar fighter plane, an improved version of the French Super-Mystere, whose engine has been replaced with the engine from a Skyhawk, an American fighter. Lt. Col. Roser was originally a Sa'ar test-pilot in the air force. When the plane's production was transferred to the Israel Aircraft Industry he went on to perform test flights there. On the maiden flight of the first Sa'ar off the production line, Roser flew the plane on the runway at the Ben-Gurion International Airport and accelerated for take-off: "It was the first take-off for the plane just off the assembly line. The Super-Mystere is an old-generation aircraft, one of the first supersonic planes produced. It is very heavy, and its engine relatively weak. I moved along the runway, gaining speed, and took off.

After take-off the plane just died - it had no strength for maneuvering, nothing. And just at the wrong time and wrong place, what do I see? A small black body moving rapidly towards me. A bird. I saw it in relative movement and suddenly it stops in front of me, and I said to myself - that's it! The last thing I managed to say was 'no!' I felt a strong blow in the large Super-Mystere air inlet. Boom! I then heard a loud explosion and there I am at almost zero altitude! I can't bailout! The ejection seat in the Super-Mystere doesn't work at low altitudes and speed. It's not like today's mechanisms that can eject you upwards even when you are stationary on the ground. In that one-hundredth of a second you have many thoughts on the possibilities of the situation: the first thought is not to bailout over a town - because at Ben-Gurion you take off right over Or Yehuda. So I turned left and again couldn't rise because I was banking, at low speed and altitude. A series of explosions started again, but I couldn't bailout because I didn't have enough speed and altitude. So I reduced the engine power, which went against all my instincts, because I actually needed maximum power in order to rise, and that's what saved me! When I reduced engine power the explosions stopped and the plane started rising slowly.

The site where the F-16 crashed on the ground in the Judean Desert.
(Photo: courtesy of the Israel Air Force)

I had to turn back to the runway as fast as possible, but I knew that if I banked left over the runway, I would pass over the airport, which means 100 to 2,000 people below. So I continued climbing, since I knew the engine was already half-dead and tried to circumvent the airport. I radioed that a bird had hit me and then a new series of explosions started, in other words, every second or two there was a very strong boom. At a certain point I decided the engine was shot anyway and it couldn't help but only endanger me. At this point I decided I had enough altitude for a tight bank and landing. The explosions were so strong, that with each one the pedals jumped under my feet. I killed the engine and had a good feeling that I would make it. I planned to touch ground at about the middle of the runway.

I landed well, stopped and got off the plane. I remember having difficulty standing, my legs barely supporting me - probably because of the excitement and tension. Many years ago I flew an Organ in the Samoa military action in Jordan. I was shot through the cockpit, hit in my face and lost one eye. I radioed in my situation and was told to bailout, but said - no way! I am bringing this plane home! That was part of our education then - there is no replacement for the craft and it had to be brought home! During all my long years flying I was hit many times, but the story with the bird is etched deep in my memory because it was the hardest. You just can't do a thing - there is no hope and you are totally helpless.

Lt. Colonel Roser received an award for "outstanding performance, distinguished flying and excellence in professional performance" for his courage and presence of mind in safely landing the "Sa'ar".

The Honey Buzzard that almost downed an "eagle"

Lt. Colonel L, a Skyhawk (called an "eagle" in the IAF) fighter pilot, flew off on a routine training flight: "I was flying at an altitude of 3,000 feet (about 1,000 meters) when suddenly I heard a loud explosion. I felt a powerful blow on my neck and didn't know what was happening to me. I was in total blackout. When I recovered a bit, I first checked to see if the plane was flying, which it was. I heard a loud noise, caused by air entering the shattered canopy. My neck was covered with blood. I didn't know if it was mine. I looked down: on the floor of the plane I saw feathers and bits of flesh. I understood that I had been hit by a bird". Lt. Colonel L managed to fly and land his aircraft at the air force base. The inquiry and examination of the feather remains showed he had been hit by a Honey Buzzard and wounded on the side of his neck. If the bird had entered the canopy 20 centimeters further right, it would have hit Lt. Colonel L in the middle of his neck and face and possibly killed him.

Two storks and an F-15 with a trail of fire 100 meters long!

A case of birdstrike almost interrupted Lt. Colonel Y's rise to his position as head of flight safety in the Israel Air Force. On 19 March 1981, at the peak of migration, during a routine day in a F-15 squadron in central Israel, Y (then a major) took-off in his plane as part of a military exercise with his squadron. About a half a minute after take-off, at an altitude of 2,500 feet (about 800 meters), Y looked down to check something in the aircraft's circuit breaker. When he raised his head, he saw he was about to collide with a large flock of storks within a few seconds! Y made a desperate but unsuccessful attempt to maneuver his plane between the storks: "As I entered the flock I bent down in the cockpit, waiting to hear the blow. A fraction of a second passed and I was sure I had escaped when I heard a very large mass hitting the aircraft. One stork collided with the plane's belly, but this was the less significant damage. The second stork entered the left engine that instantly caught fire. I immediately turned towards the base and meanwhile noticed that besides the warning light showing fire in the left engine, another one had lit to show that all the other parts were alight as well. In the F-15 this is a very serious problem - it means loss of hydraulic pressure and total loss of control over the aircraft. I tried to land on the same runway I had left a moment before. Meanwhile the engine fragments struck other hydraulic systems and the piping, cables and systems on the left side and rear of the plane caught fire. This made it almost impossible to fly the plane, already on only one engine, since I had killed the left engine the minute it caught fire. I didn't manage to land and was forced to climb so I could circle again for landing. The aircraft was barely flying. The damage to the steering system caused the plane to roll strongly to the right and a certain point I reached a situation where I was 80 degrees towards the horizon, one wing down and the other up. Another 5 degrees of inclination and I would have to bailout. At the last minute I decided to open the right burner. This worked and the plane stopped rolling at an altitude of 300 meters above the center of the base. The people below later described the situations as horrible: a completely tilted F-15 flying over the base trailing fire for 100 meters behind it. I managed to make a wide circle and started to land with the help of the brake cable. With tremendous effort, putting great pressure on the stick and with the steering system in extremely bad condition, I somehow managed to land". The experienced firefighters at the base put out the flaming plane after it stopped on the runway.

It took the Israel Air Force a year to return the aircraft to service. Following this case the plane was nicknamed the "lighter". Several months after returning to active flight, during the Lebanese War, the "lighter" lit a Syrian fighter...

The bird that downed a Kfir

Lt. Colonel K, head of the flight training unit in the Israel Air Force bailed out twice over exactly the same spot (near an air force base in northern Israel), both times from a Kfir (an IAF-improved version of the French Mirage fighter). The first time was in October 1979. K, then a major, was

A flight technician examining the hole in Col. E's Skyhawk fighter plane that was hit by a Honey Buzzard.
(Photo: courtesy of the Israel Air Force)

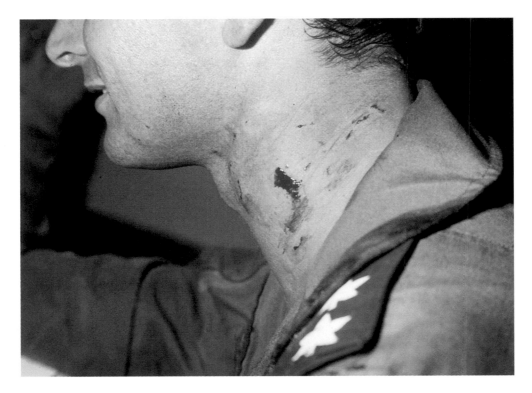

Col. E collided with a Honey Buzzard, was wounded in the neck and miraculously survived.
(upper photo: courtesy of the Israel Air Force)

The remains of the Honey Buzzard were found in Col. E's Skyhawk fighter plane.
(lower photo: courtesy of the Israel Air Force)

coming in with his plane for landing. He descended after four Phantoms (F-4) and entered a flock of migrating birds. Lt. Colonel K realized that collision was unavoidable: "I felt a strong blow and the engine power failing and saw warning lights blinking. I informed the control tower that the engine was dead and requested permission for an emergency landing. I realized immediately that there was no way I could land safely. At this point I leveled the plane, leaned over and pulled the ejection handle, but nothing happened! I bent down to see what was wrong and at that point my emotions overtook me and I started seeing pictures of my childhood in the valley over which I was flying. And then, all of a sudden, as I crouched, in the completely wrong position for bailing out, I ejected. In the seconds between pulling the handle and ejecting, I understood something was wrong, and then bailed out. I was blacked-out because of the position I was in. The first clear thought in my head after bailing out was a feeling of relief as I hung from my parachute and saw the aircraft fall. I landed on the ground with a bad feeling - I hadn't taken off to bailout. I felt terrible that four Phantoms before me landed safely and only I had been hit by a bird".

Two years later, in August 1981, Lt. Colonel K took off in a quartet for target practice: "It was the middle of August, the skies were clear and beautiful, and I was at the same spot and runway where I had bailed out before. This time there were no birds around. We returned for landing. Suddenly I heard a loud blow and the engine revolutions decreased instantly. I swore and said to myself: 'It's happening to me again'. I wasn't sure if I was dreaming or this was really happening. This time I was much calmer and went through the routine procedures to restart the engine. I informed the control tower that the engine was dead, but realized that I would be unable to perform an emergency landing. I informed the tower that I was bailing out. The first reactions after I bailed out made me feel terrible. When the base commander saw me, his first question was: 'Is this a dream or is it you again?'". The inquiry commission that examined the case discovered that the problem lay in a loosened screw that was sucked into the engine. Lt. Colonel K continued flying the Kfir with no problems, although he declared: "If I have to bailout a third time, I'll stop flying".

The Buzzard that downed a "vulture"   Brig. Gen. (res.) Israel Baharav has bitter memories of his meeting with a bird twenty-five years ago. On 19 February 1973 Baharav, then a captain, led a formation of "vultures" (the improved version of the Mirage 5), on an attack exercise in southern Israel. Baharav was flying a completely new aircraft that had logged only four flight hours before this flight. As he tells it: "We left on a training flight. We descended over the Judean Mountains to the south, following the slopes at a very low altitude. Several kilometers south of Arad (Judean Desert) we were flying at 360 knots, at an altitude of 300 feet. Suddenly, out of the corner of my eye I noticed a small, dark, spot that within a fraction of a second grew into a tremendous object! Before my brain gave the command for evasion, even before I understood what my eyes were actually seeing I felt a tremendous blow!!!

It was a gigantic bird that at the last second even spread its wings fully... It passed to my left and struck the left air inlet. The plane shook from the power of the collision. The engine made awful grinding noises, screeching and groaning, and the engine revolution clock went down wildly... I didn't need instruments to tell the engine was dead and the plane stalled in mid-air... 'Number one - you're on fire. There is a flame the length of two planes behind you!' my "number 2" reported quietly, but anxiously, on the radio. I confirm it. There is no need to tell me... all the instruments that can possibly give bad news had joined the "orchestra": the engine temperature - way up; the fire light - lit; pressures; generator; warning lights; the siren joined in deafeningly - as if I didn't know there was a "problem"...

My altitude and speed were low. Even though there seemed to be no hope or chance, I decided to try to revive the engine. I put the throttle into "off" for a second or two, activated ignition in flight and put the plane back into "neutral". There was no reaction! Meanwhile my speed is decreasing and the cockpit is filling with smoke. 'Number one abandoning!' I inform "number 2" on the radio. I have nothing left to do here anymore, in another minute the plane will crash, preferably without me...

I pulled the ejection handle. The usual second of delay... boom...boom...boom! And I am "shot" out of the plane. Through the protective veil over my face I saw

A Kfir fighter plane flying over the Judean Desert.
(Photo: Gil Arbel, courtesy of the Israel Air Force)

Brig. Gen. (res.) Israel Baharav
(Photo: Yossi Leshem)

the plane moving away. Another second passed, and the wind rolled me back... a turn...a strong pull on my shoulders and the parachute opened! I remembered that I am very close to the ground and have only a very short time before landing. A short look down made me realize that the "second act" of the play was about to start...

Up to then I had always parachuted on level ground. The surface here was mountainous, covered with cracks and crevices! The parachute swings from the ejection hadn't stopped yet, and I was swaying wildly from side to side. The strong wind dragged me and prevented me estimating my point of landing. I descended left in a "pendulum"... and... landed the length of my body on the cliff wall in one blow, as the wind spread the parachute upwards and upward.

The "third act" was easier: I left the parachute in the wadi, collected my personal equipment and climbed up the canyon waiting to be rescued."

Brig. Gen. Baharav's aircraft was almost completely burned, mainly on its right side, and dismantled completely from the fall to the ground. Feather remains and a piece of burnt flesh were found in the engine. The remains were examined at Tel-Aviv University and identified as belonging to a Buzzard species (a medium-sized bird of prey). This fit the description the pilot gave of a raptor with a wingspan of about one meter. Baharav, one of the most famous fighter pilots in the IAF, has 3 "ejections" to his name (the bird and technical problems) and shot down 12 enemy planes. In the inquiry following the accident the head of flight safety in the Israel Air Force noted that "contact was made with Tel-Aviv University and the Society for the Protection of Nature in Israel, but they have no clear map of bird movements, routes and altitudes, only conclusions based on amateur estimates with no orderly written summary. It has been agreed that these institutes would monitor and observe migration for the Israel Air Force in order to prepare more accurate maps".

Unfortunately, despite the conclusions of the head of flight safety following the accident, nothing was done to change the situation and eleven more years were to pass until cooperation with the air force was formalized and the methodical study of bird migration over Israel began.

The Brigadier that anticipated Israel Air Force Bird Plagued Zone (BPZ) Regulations

Several years before the methodical study of migration routes and timing began, and BPZ regulations forbidding low altitude flights along migration routes during the migratory season, were in effect, Brig. Gen. (res.) Yiftah Spector (a colonel at the time) was a wing commander in the Israel Air Force. He noticed that the number of collisions with birds rose significantly during the migratory season, causing severe damage. As a result, he personally instated internal BPZ regulations in his wing. He gave out instructions to his squadron flight commanders forbidding low-altitude flights, and obligating take-offs and landings at steep angles, to decrease the probability of bird-aircraft collisions.

A BPZ map was attached to these instructions. The map had many mistakes since it was not based on methodical research. Even so, there is no doubt that Colonel Spector anticipated by a half a decade the regulations that were eventually formally developed in the entire air force. He instructed squadron commanders on the importance of flight safety and the bird problem. The flight commanders did not understand the new "craze" their wing commander had adopted, and "bombarded" his office with ironic messages that tried to impress on him the importance of dealing with more "serious subjects" than migrating birds...

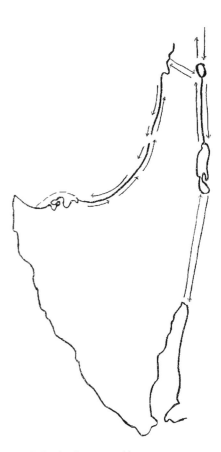

The "mistaken" map used by Colonel Spector.

The American B1-B strategic bomber.
(upper photo: courtesy of the Israel Air Force Magazine)

An American F-111 bomber whose nose was crushed by a collision with a Red-tailed Hawk.
(lower photo: courtesy of the U.S. Air Force)

C. The Conflict between Birds and Aircraft in other Parts of the World

Bird-aircraft collisions are a serious problem in many other parts of the world, not only in Israel. Air forces and civil flight authorities in the most developed countries have been compelled to devote thought, planning and means in order to find solutions to the problem.

Civilian and military air traffic has increased significantly during the last two decades. Air Forces now fly at low altitudes, both during the day and at night, using fire zones in several countries. The cost of aircraft has doubled over the last decades and the potential for damage by birds has increased dramatically.

A quick scan of the literature reveals the situation in civilian flight is similar to that in military flight. Thorpe summarized the number of civilian air collisions between 1986 and 1990 based on the ICAO IBIS System: a total of 22,331 incidents occurred in 5 years, in which 3 aircraft were destroyed and 1310 engines were damaged. Dolbeer, Wright and Cleary summarized damage caused by bird and other wildlife to civilian aircraft in the United States in 1994: based on FAA data 2150 birdstrikes were reported and 22% indicated some type of damage. An independent analysis of strike records for a major US airport estimated that fewer than 20% of all strikes were included in the FAA Wildlife Strike Database. In 1999 damage reached 240 million dollars, which means that only in the USA annual damage to civilian flights is probably close to 1 billion dollars!!

The extent of financial loss to different air forces depends on the type of aircraft used: F-15/I cost 86 million dollars each, while a Mig 21 or Skyhawk cost a "mere" few million dollars. A single pelican that collided with a B-1B strategic bomber in the USA caused $282 million in damage. In the Royal Netherlands Air Force a European Military Bird Strike Database was developed with 35,000 records of air collisions with birds from 17 different air forces (including Israel). There were over 16,000 cases of birdstrike reported in the US Air Force between 1983 and 1987, and 13,427 between 1989 and 1993 (an average of 2685 air collisions a year!). The Israel Air Force (IAF) suffered 3092 air collisions with birds in the last 25 years, an average of 258 a year, losing 8 aircraft and three pilots. In the Indian Air Force 14 jet planes and one helicopter crashed between 1980 and 1994 mainly as a result of White Headed Vultures and kites.

In many air forces data is still not collected and analyzed systematically, while many others withhold publication of data because of security regulations. For these reasons it is almost impossible to obtain an accurate global picture of the rate and number of bird collisions in military flights.

Over 50 civil aircraft have been destroyed and 190 lives lost as a result of collisions with birds or attempts to avoid them. The most serious was the Lockheed Electra case in Boston on 4 October 1960 that killed 62 people. The crash was a result of bird ingestion into three engines (starlings, weight 80 g). Multiple bird engine ingestion is still regarded as the major threat to civil aviation.

Up to and including 1994, over 170 military aircraft have been destroyed as a result of collision with birds with at least 34 occupants and 3 civilians on the ground killed. Most were single or twin engined fighter or attack aircraft. At least two cases were multiple engine ingestion in four-engined aircraft.

Between January 1995 and July 1996 four severe air collisions occurred, three of them with four-engined aircraft:

(a) On 20 January 1995 a Dassault Falcon 20 taking off from Paris Le Bourget Airport encountered a flock of Lapwings (215 g), just after rotation, and a number were ingested into the left engine. The aircraft climbed away but the pilot immediately reported that he was returning due to an engine fire. A tight left-hand circuit was flown at a height of about 500-ft AGL to land back on Runway 25. The aircraft impacted the ground just to the right to Runway 25, close to the threshold of Runway 21, was not lined up with the runway but on a heading diverging to the right by about 300. The aircraft was destroyed by impact and post impact fire. During the circuit

Remains of the American B1-B strategic bomber that crashed in September 1987 after colliding with a lone pelican. Three pilots were killed in the crash and damages reached 280 million dollars.
(Photo: courtesy of the U.S. Air Force)

July 14, 1996: E3A AWACS collided with birds while taking off at Aktion, Greece and was totally destroyed.

a number of witnesses saw the rear of the aircraft engulfed inflame. The initial investigation discovered 15 dead birds on the runway close to the point where the aircraft had become airborne. The rear cowl, exit guide vane and a number of fan blades from the left engine were found further along the runway, while the fan disk, with all its blades sheared off flush with their attachment points, was found some 500 m to the side of the runway. It has apparently been determined that, following the bird ingestion, the fan had separated and exited the engine with shrapnel penetrating the rear fuselage, puncturing the feeder tanks and a fire had then immediately broken out in this area. The accident is still under investigation.

(b) On 22 September 1995, a JT3D-engined Boeing E3 AWACS, based on the B707 4 engined airliner, was making an early morning departure from Elmdorf USAF base Anchorage, Alaska, USA. Just after the heavily loaded aircraft lifted off a large flock of Eastern Canada Geese (wt 7 kg) were encountered. Birds were ingested in engines 3 and 4, rendering the aircraft unflyable. It crashed on rising ground approximately 40 seconds later killing the 24 crew. The flock of geese was known to frequent the aerodrome and had probably been alarmed by a C130 that departed shortly before the AWACS.

(c) At Aktion Air Force Base in Greece, another Boeing AWACS was taking off on 14 July 1996. Just beyond the point of rotation a large black bird was seen close to the aircraft moving from left to right. The crew heard a noise on the right-hand side of the aircraft and the aircraft continued to accelerate for another 2-3 seconds at which point the commander initiated a rejected take-off, at a speed beyond that calculate and briefed. The aircraft over-ran the runway into a lake, resulting in the aircraft being severely damaged, the fuselage fractured etc. Of the 14 crew all escaped, one suffering back injuries. Subsequently, it was found that engine 3 had been struck (bird species unknown) but was not damaged. The commander's decision to abandon take-off was influenced by his belief the aircraft had suffered a strike in spite of a bird control program at Aktion and by his knowledge of the Alaskan accident.

(d) On 15 July 1996, a Belgian Air Force C130 Hercules was approaching Eindhoven, Netherlands. Shortly before landing, a go-around was initiated because of a large number of birds near the end of the runway. Many birds impacted the left wing area and cockpit and engines 1 and 2 lost power, but the feathered engine 3. With engine 4 at full power the aircraft turned left, lost altitude and impacted on the airfield close to the runway. A severe fire broke out but owing to lack of coordination of the fire and rescue efforts and jammed exits 35 of the 41 on board died because it had been thought that the only occupants were the four crew. Shortly before the Hercules landed a flock of birds was observed from the control tower, on and around the runway close to the tower. They were then driven away by several bird scaring rounds being fired from the tower. The flock subsequently moved away and was not observed again. Just before the aircraft landed, the bird scarer and Air Traffic Control checked the end of the runway for presence of birds but none were seen. Subsequent investigation showed that there were between 500 and 600 starlings, together with a few Lapwings, most of which were presumably in the grass around the runway. The grass had mown several days before with the cuttings still lying on the ground. If the birds were in that area, they would have been very difficult to see. It is believed the birds were scared by the approaching aircraft.

Fifty-nine people were killed in these bird collisions!!!

In September 1987, a B1-B, an American strategic bomber, took off on a low-altitude training flight over its home base in Texas. The bomber collided with a lone pelican over the La Junta area in Colorado, its fuel and hydraulic pipes burst and the plane caught fire. The crew, six pilots, navigators and system operators, lost control of the aircraft. Three of the crew successfully parachuted to safety, the remaining three were killed in the resulting crash. The aircraft cost the U.S. Air Force 280 million dollars, and with all its electronic equipment close to 500 million dollars!!

In December 1987, the President of the United State's secret Boeing 747 took off from its base in Nebraska. Immediately after take-off it suddenly collided with a flock of about 40 Snow Geese. Some of the geese were sucked into two of the 150 million dollars aircraft's four engines that ceased functioning. The nose cover split, both wings suffered serious damage and the plane was forced to return to base immediately where it crash-landed.

Fighter planes are not only hit by birds. This photograph shows the remains of a deer that collided with a U.S. Air Force Phantom at take-off. (Photo: courtesy of the U.S. Air Force)

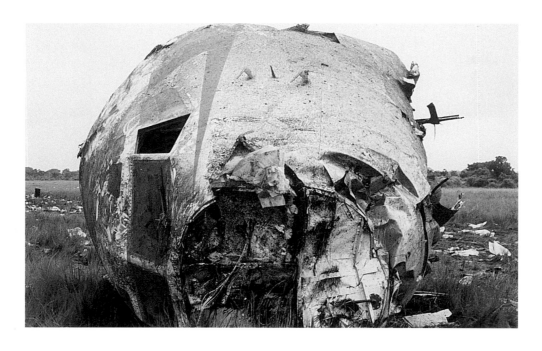

Remains of the Boeing 737 that collided with a flock of pigeons and crashed on 15 September 1988, in Ethiopia.
Thirty-five of the 104 passengers were killed.

Not only military aircraft suffer from birdstrike, many civilian planes are hit as well, mainly near airfields during take-off and landing. In most cases the damage to the aircraft is not severe and the pilot lands successfully. But in some cases the accidents are very serious, leading to loss of life, as can be seen from the following:

On 4 June 1960, a Lockheed L188, flying above the Boston Airport in the United States, collided with a flock of Starlings that were drawn into its engines. The aircraft stalled and crashed. Sixty-two of the 72 passengers and crew were killed and nine others were seriously injured.

On 15 September 1988, a Boeing 737 took off from the Bahar Dar Airport in Ethiopia and collided with a flock of Speckled Pigeons that were drawn into two of the engines putting them out of commission. The pilots tried to return to the airport, but when they saw this would be impossible tried to crash land in an open area. The plane hit a riverbank when it landed and caught fire. Thirty-five of the 104 passengers and crew were killed and twenty-one were severely injured.

Flight authorities in many countries, realizing the danger posed by birds near airports, have used various means in order to chase the birds away. Vegetation has been cleared and marshes and water bodies drained in order to eliminate food sources that might attract birds. Various devices have been tried to frighten off birds, such as flags and signs bearing raptor-like shapes, gas cannons that make blasting sounds and others. These methods have also been used in various military airfields. The Israel Air Force established a special unit whose purpose is to prevent bird problems near bases. These tactics have improved the situation near the bases, but have not solved the problem along flight routes in different parts of the country.

July 15, 1996: Remains of a Belgian C-130 Hercules that collided with a flock of starlings at Eindhoven, The Netherlands, killing 35 people and wounding 6.

This flock of starlings, which was photographed over Tel-Aviv, Israel, may cause severe damage to large passenger aircraft.
(Photo: Jonathan Shaul)

"Frozen fowl" on a direct flight from JFK

On 17 November 1996 El-Al flight no. 014 (B-747) left from New York to Ben-Gurion Airport. When taking off the captain heard a bang on the right side of the aircraft, but everything was in order so the flight continued as planned. After landing at Ben-Gurion a large seagull was found to have hit the base of the right wing, crashing through the glass covering the wing lights (8-mm thick) entering the wing. The seagull broke an avian flight record when it covered about 11,000 kilometers in less than ten hours, all this at a temperature of -60ºC. Unfortunately this "frozen fowl" was not kosher.

Remains of the seagull that came on the direct flight from New York to Israel on 18 November 1996 via an El-Al Boeing 747 and what was left of the shattered glass.
(photo: Yossi Leshem)

On 12 November 1975, an American Airlines DC-10 aircraft collided with a flock of seagulls while taking-off in JFK airport. The aircraft burned out completely but all of the 139 passengers managed to escape safely.

Page 130:
The motorized glider following a flock of White Storks.
(Drawing: James P. Smith)

Chapter 4
The Study of Bird Migration in Israel

גַּם־חֲסִידָה בַשָּׁמַיִם יָדְעָה מוֹעֲדֶיהָ וְתֹר וְסִיס וְעָגוּר שָׁמְרוּ אֶת־עֵת בֹּאָנָה (ירמיהו ח׳, ז)

"Yea, the stork in the heaven
Knoweth her appointed times;
And the turtledove and the swift and the crane
Observe the time of their coming"
                                        (Jeremiah 8:7)

A. The History of Bird Migration Study

Although the phenomenon of bird migration was known to many throughout the ancient world, its methodical study started only towards the middle of the 19th century. Early attempts at marking birds however, started much earlier: about 750 years ago a German monk attached a small piece of parchment to the leg of a swallow taken from its nest. On it he wrote: "Swallow, where do you reside in winter?" In spring the swallow returned to its nest with a new piece of parchment on its leg, and on it was written: "In Asia, in the house of Petrus". This is apparently the earliest known case of "scientific" bird ringing (banding) known.

At the end of the 16th century a Peregrine belonging to Henry IV, king of France, was ringed with a gold ring, but escaped from the king's palace at Fountainebleau, near Paris. It was found several days later on the island of Malta in the Mediterranean, 2,160 kilometers from its place of captivity. In 1770, a heron with rings on its legs was found in Germany. On the rings was an inscription that said the rings had been put on the heron in Turkey several years earlier. One of the noblemen who escaped Paris at the outbreak of the French Revolution in 1789, hid in his castle in the Lorraine region in eastern France. He put a metal ring on one of a pair of swallows nesting in the castle and found that the swallow returned to its nest for three consecutive years.

A permanent mesh trap for catching birds for ringing at Fair Isle in the Shetlands.
(Photo: Ofer Bahat)

Thompson, a British missionary who lived in Syria and Israel for 30 years in the 19th century, described stork migration in Israel in his memoirs. He was very impressed by the tremendous numbers of passing storks and recounts that in 1846, during spring migration, one of the weakened storks landed on a mountain near Safed (in the Upper Galilee) and was trapped. The trappers were surprised to find a silver ornament on the stork's neck and took it to the governor who sent it on to the Turkish Pasha in Acre, who passed it on to the British consul in Beirut. The ornament contained a letter from Octavia, the young Countess of Gotzen in Germany who wrote that the stork had nested for years on the tower of her castle, but the tower had collapsed and wounded it. The countess tended the stork, and after it recovered attached the silver necklace to its neck and released it with other migrating storks. The letter included a plea to whoever found the stork to send the necklace to the countess at all costs, since she was very curious to know its migration route. The British consul wrote the countess with details of the stork's adventures and received a warm thank-you letter in return.

From the second half of the 19th century, bird migration research took a big step forward when scientific methods and systematic information gathering started. Researchers examined stuffed bird collections and according to the finding date and geographic location received a fair idea on the location of breeding and wintering areas. At this same time ornithology began developing as a special field which attracted researchers and nature lovers. In Heligoland, a small island in the North Sea, north of the German coast, Gatke, a German researcher, established an observatory for following bird migration. He devoted fifty years of his life to observing and tracking at Heligoland and described no less than 398 different bird species that were seen on the tiny island during his years of research!

In the western part of the North Sea, east of the Scottish coast, British ornithologists began visiting Fair Isle. This small island, located on the principal migration route between northern Europe and the British Isles, soon became one of the leading sites for birdwatchers from all England. Just as in Heligoland, here too there was a

Page 132:
A castle tower in Germany where five pairs of White Storks nest.
(Photo: Pierre Perrin)

tremendous amount and variety of bird species, including some very rare in England. Systematic ringing of migrating birds began and large mesh traps were used to catch the birds. About a hundred years later, in 1948, a small bird observatory for watching migrating birds was established for researchers and wardens and a small hotel for visitors to the island.

In the 19th century the first interlinked information gathering systems based on birdwatchers and ornithologists were established. In England in 1834, an observer network was established along the coast to report migratory movements of sea birds. Similar observation networks were established at other sites in Europe. Questionnaires and report forms were sent to birdwatchers all over the continent, which they would complete and return to the data centers. In North America, across the Atlantic Ocean, extensive efforts to gather information on birds began in the second half of the 19th century. In 1883 the American Ornithological Union was established and one of its first working committees dealt with gathering information on migration.

During the 20th century migration research took a giant leap forward. In many places along migration routes in Europe and North America observatories were established to study and ring migrating birds. Nevertheless, it was only from the middle of the 20th century that modern technology was applied in the study of migration. The development of light, rapid aircraft, of radar and of powerful miniature radio transmitters furnished important techniques for learning about migration routes, altitude, estimating migration magnitude more accurately, and tracking it during the day, night and in all weather conditions.

B. Bird Ringing

A Steppe Buzzard in Eilat with a ring on its leg.
(Photo: Ofer Bahat)

Bird ringing or banding, in which an aluminum ring is fitted on one of a bird's legs, has been one of the most common methods of studying migration since the 19th century. Its principal advantage is its simplicity and the reliable information it provides. Rings come in different sizes for different species, and care is taken to use one large enough not to pinch the leg, causing friction and possible injury, but small enough not to interfere with normal activity. The ring is inscribed with an individual serial number and the name of the ringing institute. Bird ringing provides information on when and where a bird was ringed and eventually on where and when it was found. In both cases, information on the area where the bird was found, the habitat, what condition it was in (alive, dead and how it died - shot, hit by a car, etc. - found freshly dead or long dead, etc.), is recorded. This information allows us to determine at least two sites on the bird's migration route. In cases where the bird was ringed at the nest, ringing information can provide data on the site along the migration route or on the bird's winter quarters.

Bird ringers are specialists in their field and can ring birds only after special training and with an appropriate permit. They must have extensive experience in using the mist nets used for trapping birds, in extracting birds from the nets (without injuring them), identifying the birds in the hand, ringing and releasing them. Most ringers devote many weeks (or even months) every year to ringing birds.

In Israel too, there are several dozen accomplished ringers with extensive experience. Ringing in Israel is supervised by the Israel Bird Ringing Center which is operated jointly by the Society for the Protection of Nature in Israel and the Israel Nature Reserves Authority. The ringing center sells ringing equipment, compiles the data recorded by ringers and provides information on ringing recoveries. Shalom Suaretz established the first ringing station in the country in the late 1960's at Ma 'agan Mikhael on the coast. The station was active for many years but is now closed. There are three permanent ringing stations currently active in the country. The largest is also the oldest that was established by Bruria Gal in the late 1960's in the fields of Kibbutz Eilot, north of Eilat, in southern Israel. Many other ringers followed, and today the International Birdwatching Center in Eilat (IBCE) runs the station. It organizes tours for the many birdwatchers in the area that can visit the ringing station and watch the ringers at work. In the 1980's William S. Clark, working for the Israel

A ring fitted on the leg of a Steppe Eagle in Eilat.
(Photo: Yossi Eshbol - SPNI Collection)

Pages 136-137:
Only in Eilat, at the junction of three continents, can an American bird ringer (Katy Duffy), release a Steppe Eagle
from Russia, as part of a research project in Israel organized by the Israel Raptor Information Center.
(Photo: Yossi Eshbol - SPNI Collection)

Raptor Information Center (IRIC), set up a special ringing station for trapping migrating birds of prey. Edna Gorney followed Clark and was later replaced by Reuven Yosef, the current director of the IBCE. The second ringing station, in the Rose Garden adjacent to Israel's Knesset, is probably the most unique - the only one in the world located within the boundaries of a parliament. The green expanses surrounding the Knesset (Israel's parliament) attract many tired migrants who converge on this green spot in the heart of built-up Jerusalem. Amir Balaban and Gideon Perlman have been ringing at the site for over ten years, but only in 1998 did it become a permanent station open to thousands of tourists and other visitors. The third station is at Kibbutz Kfar Ruppin in the Bet She'an Valley in northern Israel. The kibbutz established a birdwatching center along with the SPNI as a tourist attraction visited by thousands of adults and schoolchildren every year. These three stations are open seven months a year during the migration seasons.

Ringers and ringing centers the world over are in close contact and exchange ringing information. One of the problems with bird ringing is the low percentage of recoveries. In order to improve the situation, many ringers work jointly to trap and release ringed birds at different sites along migration routes to gain better understanding of the exact routes the birds take. Cooperative projects of this sort have been organized along the United States coast and by ringers working the Baltic Sea area.

It is not always necessary to trap a bird in order to read its ring number - large rings can sometimes be read from afar by telescope. Georg Fiedler, a German ornithologist, reads stork rings and other bird rings with a telescope, from close quarters, while in a vehicle, to avoid frightening the birds. He has visited Israel several times, and provided information on European storks wintering or migrating in Israel. Between 1981 and 1995, Fiedler read the rings of more than 30 storks in

Bird Ringing Recoveries Map

Recoveries of Pied Wagtails, Barn Swallow, White Storks and Steppe Buzzards ringed in Israel, or ringed elsewhere and recovered in Israel.

1. Barn Swallow ringed in Nir David, Israel and recovered in Malawi.
2. Barn Swallow ringed in Bulgaria and recovered in Bareqet, Israel.
3. Barn Swallow ringed in Bareqet, Israel and recovered in South Africa.
4. Barn Swallow ringed in Bareqet, Israel and recovered in Zaire.
5. Barn Swallow ringed in Bareqet, Israel and recovered in Russia.
6. White Stork ringed in Yugoslavia and recovered in Tse'elim, Israel.
7. White Stork ringed in Poland and recovered in Ma'agan Mikhael, Israel.
8. White Stork ringed in Germany and recovered in Nir David, Israel.
9. White Stork ringed in Germany and recovered in Maoz Haim, Israel.
10. White Stork ringed in Denmark and recovered in Neve Etan, Israel.
11. Steppe Buzzard ringed in Finland and recovered in Bet Alfa, Israel.
12. Steppe Buzzard ringed in Eilat, Israel and recovered in South Africa.
13. Steppe Buzzard ringed in Eilat, Israel and recovered in Russia.
14. Steppe Buzzard ringed in Eilat, Israel and recovered in Armenia.
15. Steppe Buzzard ringed in Eilat, Israel and recovered in Namibia.
16. Steppe Buzzard ringed in Tse'elim, Israel and recovered in Russia.
17. Pied Wagtail ringed in Ma'agan Mikhael, Israel and recovered in Lithuania.
18. Pied Wagtail ringed in Sweden and recovered in Taibeh, Israel.
19. Pied Wagtail ringed in Eilat, Israel and recovered in Norway.
20. Pied Wagtail ringed in Eilat, Israel and recovered in Sweden.

(Drawing: Tuvia Kurtz)

138

Israel. Some of these were ringed as nestlings in Germany and wintered in the Bet-She'an Valley fish ponds, others came from Czechoslovakia, Poland and Hungary. Storks ringed in Czechoslovakia, Germany and northern Greece have been found in the Ma'agan-Mikhael area.

One of the White Storks wintering in the Bet-She'an Valley in December 1982 had been ringed as an adult at the nest in July 1978, on an island in the Elbe River in Germany. This stork was seen again at its nest in Germany year after year, until 1984. It was seen once again in winter 1983, at the same site it had been found before. Unfortunately, in the winter of 1985, it was found dead in the Bet-She'an Valley, lying in a pond with a broken wing. Ringing data showed it to be a male that had paired with a 19-year old (!) female and together they succeeded in raising 4-5 young each year. This data illustrates the vast amount of information that can be obtained from observations of ringed birds, on breeding site fidelity, wintering site fidelity and the age of birds living in the wild.

Ringing provides interesting and important information on birds whose rings cannot be read from afar as well. The following cases of birds of prey ringed or recovered in Israel illustrate the importance of the information obtained from ringing: A Buzzard ringed in Eilat in March 1985 was found in December 1986 in South Africa, 7,150 kilometers from its ringing site. Another Buzzard ringed in Eilat in April 1969 was found in October 1972 in southern Siberia, about 4,400 kilometers from its ringing site. A Buzzard ringed in Finland on 5 November 1978 was found wounded about 4 months later on 5 June 1978 at Bet-Alfa. This Buzzard covered a distance of 3,100 kilometers between its ringing and recovery sites. A Pallid Harrier ringed in Eilat in April 1985 was found four years later, in April 1989, in the Chad Lake area in western Africa, 3,200 kilometers away from its ringing site. Another Pallid Harrier ringed in Eilat in April 1985, was found about four and a half years later, in September 1989, in the area of the Jordan-Iraq border. An Osprey ringed in Finland on 15 July 1983 was found two months later, on 18 September 1983, at Nahshonim, about 3,400 kilometers from its ringing site.

It is clear from all the above that ringing is a powerful means of studying migration, providing important, accurate information. Its major disadvantage is that it is at best partial, and in most cases allows us to identify only two points along the ringed bird's migration route.

The Pied Wagtail on the Sweden-Haifa "line"

Ya'akov Langer is one of the oldest, most experienced bird ringers in Israel. On 19 February 1986 he set up mist nets to trap passerines at the Meqorot water reservoir near the Haifa sewage treatment plant and was pleasantly surprised: a Pied Wagtail with a Swedish ring was caught in the net. Ya'akov added an Israeli ring to the bird's other leg and released it. The Swedish ringing center informed him that the wagtail was a male ringed at the nest on the island of Gotland in southeast Sweden, on 24 June 1983. In the summer of 1986, several months after the wagtail was caught in Israel, it was retrapped in Sweden. On 15 February 1987 the wagtail was once again caught by Ya'akov Langer in exactly the same spot it had been found the year before! The Swedish wagtail apparently migrates south each year from its breeding quarters in Sweden to winter in the reservoir near Haifa, flying about 3,000 kilometers in each direction! The wagtail was last seen in the winter of 1987 in Israel, which means it lived at least 4 years, during which it migrated between Sweden and Israel, flying 6,000 kilometers annually, a total distance of 24,000 kilometers!

The "mystic" tale of the Slovakian Imperial Eagle

On 19 December 1986, William S. Clark and Hadoram Shirihai saw a ringed Imperial Eagle while ringing wintering raptors in the western Negev in Israel, in a project organized by the SPNI's Raptor Information Center. The Imperial Eagle, a rare winter visitor to Israel, has a wingspan that can reach 2.1 meters. After three days Clark and Shirihai succeeded in trapping the eagle and reading the inscription on its ring - LM-6486 - from the National Museum at Prague. There are only 15-20 pairs of Imperial Eagles breeding throughout the Czech Republic and Slovakia. This made this finding even more amazing, since the probability of a ringed bird of this species reaching Israel is minimal. Two months after the eagle was released in Israel, the Slovakian ringing center returned information on the ringed eagle: it was a female ringed as a chick at the nest in the Carpathian Mountains on 10 July 1986 (about five months before it was found in Israel) by Dr. Stefan Danko.

The Slovakian scientist wrote his colleagues in Israel that it was an inspiring experience to receive regards from this rare eagle he had ringed, even more so since they came from 2,500 kilometers away. He was happy to learn that Israel was a safe wintering area for Slovakian eagles and sent a photo taken of the eagle as a chick in the nest.

Yossi Leshem was very excited by Dr. Danko's letter. From it he learned that the eagle had been ringed close to where Dr. Danko lived, in Michaelovce, a small town of about 10,000 inhabitants in eastern Slovakia. This was the town where Yossi's parents-in-law were born, and from where his father-in-law had immigrated to Israel from there 53 years before the Imperial Eagle! In this manner the eagle closed a "mystic circle", not to mention the fact that this was the first time his father-in-law started taking a serious interest in raptor migration...

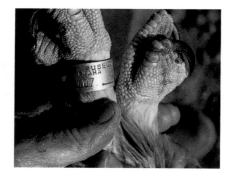

The ring from the National Museum in Prague on the leg of the Imperial Eagle trapped in Israel.
(Photo: Hadoram Shirihai)

The Imperial Eagle photographed in its nest in Slovakia on 10 July 1986 by Dr. Stefan Danko.

140

The Slovakian Imperial Eagle upon release in the western Negev on 19 December 1986.
(upper photo: William S. Clark)

A Short-toad Eagle shading its chick at the nest.
(lower photo: Stefan Danko)

A Bedouin sheik from the Dimona area in the Negev, watches the work of SPNI ornithologists and Israel Air Force birdwatchers with interest, during the spring soaring bird migration survey in the Negev.
(Photo: Yossi Leshem)

hour and minimum speed 82 kilometers per hour (with the engine on). All these make it the optimal solution for monitoring soaring birds. It seats two people, side by side, at the front. The propeller is located behind the canopy so both observers have a very wide, unimpeded field of vision. The glider can carry 250 kilograms, so two people, the pilot and a birdwatcher, and about 30 liters of fuel can be carried, allowing 4 and a half flight hours with the engine running. In order to enable flights the length of Israel, a spare fuel tank, with an electrically activated pump was attached to the glider, making it possible to spend up to 9 continuous hours in the air. When a migrating flock was located the glider pilot could kill the engine and glide and soar wing to wing with the birds.

The motorized glider is equipped with flying instruments that allowed migrating flocks velocity and altitude at every stage of the flight from the point of entering the thermal (thermal base) to leaving it for gliding (thermal crest), flight direction and rate of climb and glide, to be measured accurately. Flight data for bird flocks was recorded on special forms or on tape. Each time the flock entered a thermal from a glide the coordinates of the thermal were recorded, as well as the time the first birds entered it and their altitude. When the first birds left the thermal and began gliding again, time, altitude and the new coordinates (in cases where there was horizontal drift that deflected the crest of the thermal relative to its base) were recorded again.

Flocks were located by ground observers or by the approach radar at the Ben-Gurion International Airport. With the first method, one of the survey team coordinators would drive around and look for flock roosts each evening. In spring there were several preferred roosting sites. Storks, for example, were seen almost every evening roosting in several kibbutz fields: Revivim, Tse'elim, Urim in the western Negev. In autumn pelicans prefer the Hula Nature Reserve and Kfar Barukh reservoir in the Jezreel Valley and the Zebulun Valley; Honey Buzzards and Lesser Spotted Eagles the pine groves in the Giv'at Hamoreh area, Nazereth and Koah Forest, and storks the fish ponds in the Bet-She'an Valley. The glider flight plan for the following day was determined according to information received nightly by the survey coordinators. Only flocks with at least 500 individuals were tracked, to facilitate their location both from the glider and by radar. By this method we succeeded in following pre-determined migrating flocks daily, in autumn from northern Israel to the Egyptian border and in spring, in the opposite direction.

With the second method the glider waited at one of several airfields: Ben-Gurion, Atarot or Sede Dov, and when the migrating flock was located on the radar by the controllers at Ben-Gurion they directed the glider to it, until eye contact was made with the flock. At this point the glider attached itself to the flock and escorted it along its entire flight route. Birds of prey become accustomed to the glider escorting them on their flight easily. Storks take about an hour to accept the glider presence, while pelicans never get used to it and are frightened by the glider. As a result, when the glider accompanied a pelican flock, it kept at least 100 meters away in order not to disturb the birds and affect their natural behavior.

The observer in the glider would count the individuals in the migrating flock. These counts helped calibrate the radar picture at Ben-Gurion International Airport. After dozens of calibration flights it became possible to estimate the number of birds in a flock from the radar screen, with a reasonable degree of accuracy.

Since the soaring birds flew routes outside normal approved flight lanes in Israel and posed a threat to the Israel Air Force, the glider pilot received special permission to fly freely anywhere, while the air force control system cleared the area of other planes crossing the path of the birds. A total of 173 successful tracking flights in the motorized glider took place during the study, adding up to 720 flight hours. Approximately half the tracking hours were carried out in spring and half in autumn.

A self-portrait photographed in the motorized glider while tracking migration. On the right - Mikhael Pinkus, one of the glider pilots, on the left - Yossi Leshem.
(Photo: Yossi Leshem)

The instrument panel in the glider provides accurate data on flight speed, altitude, direction and climb and glide rates. On the right are Yossi Leshem's knees, between them the stick and on his left the notebook in which data was recorded. On the left is Eli Peretz's, the glider pilot, hand.
(Photo: Yossi Leshem)

F. Unmanned Aircraft (Drone)

The Israel Aircraft Industry and the Tadiran Company developed the Drone, a small unmanned-aircraft, as part of a military system. It is flown by remote control from a ground-based system in a control vehicle. Two people control the system: one flies the Drone and the other works the various systems carried by it, that include a complex video camera, a night vision system, communications and relay equipment and various other instruments. The Drone can fly ranges up to 200 kilometers and remain in the air for 4-5 consecutive hours, reaching a velocity of approximately 60 knots (about 110 kilometers per hour). The pictures transmitted by the video camera can be received from distances up to 200 kilometers from the control vehicle. The complex video camera has a zoom lens that can focus on distant pictures or photograph wide-angle pictures. The advanced capability of the camera, combined with the Drone's slow flight and its ability to remain aloft while photographing what is happening on the ground continuously, allowed the Drone to fly at an altitude of 6000-7000 feet (about 2000-2300 meters) while photographing migrating birds several thousand feet below it, without disturbing them, and without the birds knowing that an intricate camera was photographing their migration route.

On a preliminary flight to test the Drone's ability to track a soaring bird flock in autumn 1986, it succeeded in locating a flock of 50 pelicans over the Sea of Galilee and flying south with the flock, at an altitude of 4,000-5,000 feet a distance of 45 kilometers, to Tirat Tsvi. Following this trial, an agreement was reached with the Israel Defense Forces Intelligence Unit to use Drones for tracking migrating birds. The flights were planned to coincide with training flights for Drone operator teams. The methods used were similar to those used with the motorized glider. Birdwatching teams on the ground located stork, pelican or raptor flocks landing to roost the evening before the planned flight. When the flocks were located, a flight was set for the next day, and the researcher sat with the operators in the control vehicle. The Drone was directed to the flock while the ground observers signaled the site of the roosting flock with a white sheet spread on the ground.

After taking off, the Drone would attach itself to a bird flock and fly with it, high above. In this manner the entire flight route was recorded by the video camera, while a computerized map was being plotted in the control vehicle. The major advantages of using a Drone are that it provides at least five tracking hours in the air; its complex video photography enables focusing on a small number of birds and continuously monitoring their behavior while flying (which had not been possible from the glider); its ability to fly slowly is extremely suitable for tracking soaring birds and the fact that it can monitor birds from high altitudes ensures migrating flocks are not disturbed. Another distinct advantage is the fact that Drone flight ability is almost unaffected by weather condition. Despite its complexity and its great capability in tracking migrating birds, the Drone had several limitations that emerged during the study: it must track the flock continuously, since if a flock is lost, even for several minutes, due to operator error or any other reason, the chances of re-locating it are minimal; when there is partial cloudiness, the area below the Drone is hidden and its spotting ability diminished; the Drone cannot provide altitude data, although by comparing the size of the birds in the photo to the size of objects on the ground (such as cars), altitude can be calculated reasonably accurately. In addition flight coordination is complicated, and as a result of all these, the use of the Drone was relatively limited compared to the motorized glider.

The current study is the first biological study in the world that used an unmanned aircraft - an army intelligence instrument - for research, or in other words, the modern 20th century version of the prophecy of Isaiah: "...And they shall beat their swords into plowshares..." (Isaiah 4:2) is coming true.

G. Radar

Despite Israel's unique location on the soaring bird migration route, and the great advantages of using radar in migration research, this method was not used in Israel for migration study until 1985.

Radar was developed for military purposes, to control air traffic and detect aircraft. Various bodies such as metals, clouds, raindrops, birds and even insects reflect

The Drone control vehicle.
(upper photo)
The Drone in flight.
(lower photo).
(Courtesy of the Israel Aircraft Industry)

Page 149:
An F-16 fighter plane over mount Tabbor.
(Photo: Duby Tal, Albatross Inc.)

electromagnetic waves transmitted into space. The various objects echoing radar transmissions interfere with the original purpose of the radar (airplane detection), but as a result make radar a first rate research instrument, excellent for detecting birds. The radar's greatest advantages are its ability to detect both diurnal and nocturnal migration and track migration at altitudes beyond the visual range of even the best equipped ground-based observers. As a result several studies using radar to track migrating birds have been done during the last decades.

Every body moving through the atmosphere has a radar cross-section (RCS). The RCS is based on several factors such as the body's mass, surface area and the materials it is composed of. Birds reflect radar echoes due to the highly polarized water molecules in their body (which is the reason the majority of radar echoes are reflected off the bird's body and not its wings). As a result, large soaring birds with a large body mass, such as storks, pelicans and raptors, reflect radar echoes better than small birds do. During the present study the Israel Air Force needed real-time information on the presence of birds in Israel's air space. Radar for this purpose had to be able to detect relatively slow-moving objects such as birds, and cover a large part of the air space over the country. Eight different radar were tested, and only two were found appropriate for this study: the approach radar at Ben-Gurion International Airport and the weather forecast radar in the Nitzana area.

The approach radar at Ben-Gurion International Airport, an ASR-8 (Airport Surveillance Radar) manufactured by Texas Instruments has been used by the Israel Airport Authority since1983. It was developed specifically for controlling approaching airport traffic and is the most common radar at airports in the United States, and considered one of the best of its kind. In autumn of 1985 preliminary tests of the radar's ability to identify bird flocks were done. Lt. Col. (Res.) Pini Magor, who had extensive experience working with radar systems in the air force, Yossi Leshem and Ilana Agat were in charge of the tests. Flocks of migrating birds were detected on the radar screen as early as the first days of observation. In spring 1986 the radar was used for several days to track migration, this time using the motorized glider, light aircraft and ground observers to confirm its ability to identify flocks of migrating birds. A detailed work plan was formulated with the Israel Airport Authority staff and the controllers at Ben-Gurion International Airport for autumn 1986. The airport authority allotted one of the radar screens in the control tower to the study during the entire migration season, seven months a year. The Israel Air Force placed women soldiers to staff the radar screen during all hours of the day. Major A, a reserve officer in the control unit, coordinated the work. The radar screen was photographed every 15 minutes. At the same time the screen was photographed the soldiers drew the picture shown on the screen manually, adding wind data and direction, migration magnitude and the bird's location.

Results showed that this method allowed flocks comprising 1000 birds and more to be detected, from a range of 40 miles (about 73 kilometers). On days when soaring conditions were good, and the flocks flew at an altitude of 5000 feet (about 1700 meters) or higher, they were located at distances up to 50 miles. On most days flocks could be located within ranges of at least 30 to 35 miles. The radar covered the area between the Ma'agan-Mikhael - Afula line in the north, and the Bet-Kama - Gaza line in the south, thus allowing methodical tracking of all soaring bird flocks flying west of the central mountain range (Israel's water divide). The radar could detect flocks migrating over the Jordan Valley only if they rose above the peaks of the Judean Mountains.

Migrating flocks were located on the radar screen with a cursor and the rate and progress direction of the flock tracked for five minutes. In autumn most flocks migrate south or south-southwest and in spring the direction is reversed by 180°. their progress rate (as found from glider flights) is between 30 and 50 k.p.h., so they can be easily located. With experience, flocks were identified immediately on the screen. There was no problem distinguishing aircraft from bird flocks, since every airplane has an electronic identification number that appears on the radar screen and moves with the plane's echo on the screen. In order to test radar reliability and its ability to locate soaring bird flocks over 40 motorized glider and Cessna flights were flown in autumn 1986. The control officer directed the researcher in the glider towards the flock, and when it was spotted the birds in it were counted. At the same

The Drone flying with a migrating flock. (Courtesy of the Israel Aircraft Industry)

Chapter 5
Study Results

אַךְ־שָׁם נִקְבְּצוּ דַיּוֹת אִשָּׁה רְעוּתָהּ (ישעיהו ל״ד, טו)

"Yea, there shall the kites be gathered"
(Isaiah, 34:15)

A migrating Lesser Spotted Eagle - photographed from the motorized glider.
(Photo: Kobi Rahmilevitz)

Honey Buzzard, Levant Sparrowhawk, Lesser Spotted Eagle, Black Kite and others. Hundreds of thousands of Steppe Buzzards, for example, pass over the Eilat Mountains in spring, while in autumn at the most only a few thousand can be seen. Seasonal variations in migration can be understood only if the subject is examined on a broad scale. A similar seasonal difference between migration routes is also found in other avian orders, such as passerines and waders. This difference seems implausible at first, since the birds leave a given breeding site somewhere in northern Europe or Asia and fly off to the same wintering site in Africa year after year. Seasonal variations in migration routes are caused by several factors such as changes in weather, wind regime and availability of food sources along the migration route. Another explanation for route change claims that the key factor in route choice is the avoidance of sea-crossings, since no thermals are formed over water and soaring conditions are very bad. The geographic location of the different species' breeding grounds in relation to Israel's longitude (350) evidently plays a major role in determining the migration route in autumn and spring as can be seen from the following cases:

The Lesser Spotted Eagle, 95% of whose breeding grounds are found west of Israel, flies over Israel in autumn only on the western route, along the western slopes of the mountains. The entire world population of this species apparently uses this route in autumn, while in spring the entire population seems to use the Negev - Dead Sea - Jordan Valley route. The entire population of the Levant Sparrowhawk, whose range lies between the 20th and 52nd meridian (so that Israel's longitude crosses the center of its range) migrates over Israel. In autumn it passes over the western slopes of the mountains, while in autumn it flies north from Eilat over the Arava, the Jordan Valley and the Hula Valley. The range of the White Stork that migrates via the eastern Mediterranean lies between the 11th and 50th meridian, although most storks breed west of the 35th meridian. It seems that the entire population of these storks passes over Israel in spring. In autumn, however, as a result of climatic factors, about 45% of the population fly over the Jordan Valley in Israel, while the rest pass over further east, probably over Jordan. Some of the storks migrating over Jordan turn southwest into Israel in the area of the Jordan Valley, Dead Sea and Arava.

The Honey Buzzard has an extremely large range and the population migrating via the eastern Mediterranean Basin breeds between the 15th and 90th meridian. As a result only part of the global population presumably migrates through Israel in autumn, along the western and eastern slopes of the central mountain range. In spring most of the migrating population converges over the Eilat Mountains and flies northeast from there to its breeding quarters. In 1985 851,598 Honey Buzzards were counted - the largest number ever! This supports the assumption that roughly a third to one half of the world population passes over Israel in autumn and spring.

The Steppe Eagle is the only species nesting east of Israel between the 41st and 122nd meridian. Its nesting area is relatively southern and includes central Asia, so that this species migrates on an unusual route in a general east-west direction from Asia to Africa. As a result, Steppe Eagles can be seen in the Eilat area in similar numbers both in spring and autumn. It is estimated that these numbers comprise about one-third of the world population. In spring 28,134 Steppe Eagles were counted in the Eilat area, and in autumn - 24,246. Part of the population migrates north of Eilat in autumn continuing through Sinai towards Suez in Egypt, where 64,880 eagles were counted. Another part of the population migrates east of Eilat, crossing the Red Sea at the Bab-al-Mandab Straits, where up to 67,586 eagles were counted in autumn. In spring 1985, 75,073 Steppe Eagles were counted over Eilat, an unusually large number, which confirms the numbers counted in Bab-al-Mandab and Suez.

A Spotted Eagle resting during migration.
(Photo: Yig'al Livneh)

D. Flight Speed and other Characteristics

Soaring bird flight altitude depends on soaring conditions in the area. Thermals develop differently during different hours of the day according to the heating of the ground. Maximal thermal development usually occurs between 11:00 A.M. and 4:00 P.M. and most soaring birds reach maximal altitudes during noon hours. Data on soaring bird flight altitude and speed were first recorded in Israel during this study using the motorized glider, light aircraft and Drone. The most accurate data was recorded by the motorized glider. Altitude data includes the flight altitude at which the birds entered the thermal on which they soared, their altitude at the upper edge of the thermal, and the altitude loss before entering the next thermal. The aerial distance the birds covered, including climb, loss of altitude and progress rate was calculated. The average flight altitude for different soaring bird species above the ground was collected with the motorized glider from thousands of thermals and compared. The White Pelican that weighs the most, and so has the largest wing load, migrates at the lowest altitude, between 344 and 562 meters above ground, and at the slowest average velocity - 29.2 kilometers per hour. Its average climb time within a thermal is the longest - 4.6 minutes, and accordingly, the average number of thermals it exploits an hour is the smallest - 4.6.

The White Stork has a lower wing load than the Pelican, migrates at a higher altitude, between 463 and 731 meters above ground, and its average migration speed is 38.7 kilometers per hour. Its average climb time in thermals is 3.4 minutes and the average number of thermals it exploits in an hour accordingly larger - 5.7.

The Lesser Spotted Eagle is smaller and lighter than the White Stork and migrates even higher, at an altitude of 567 to 871 meters above ground and at an average flight speed of 50.9 kilometers per hour. The Honey Buzzard is the smallest and lightest in this group and has the lowest wing load. It migrates at the highest altitude level (836-1,123 meters above ground), climbs the fastest in thermals (2.2 minutes) and the number of thermals it exploits per hour is the highest - 5.7.

The Levant Sparrowhawk, whose weight and size are even smaller than the Honey Buzzard, migrates at the highest altitude level. Its speed however, made it impossible to track its flocks with the motorized glider.

E. Daily and Seasonal Progress Rate

When examining daily and seasonal progress in soaring birds, we must take into account that the bird has to find the optimal progress rate in relation to its aerodynamic structure and gliding conditions. Flight speed that is too high can deplete energy reserves and cause overheating. Flight speed that is too low wastes precious time and can prevent the migratory journey being completed in time. Thus, the optimal progress rate is a compromise between the need to cover maximal distances in a given time and the need to save energy and reduce the power needed for flying to a minimum.

The progress rate of soaring birds from one thermal to another is dependent on the glide coefficient, the ratio between the horizontal distance covered by the bird and its altitude loss in the same time unit. The force of rising air currents between thermals also has a major effect. A soaring bird will cover the longest horizontal distance when gliding at its highest glide rate. This condition is met when the force of upcurrents is maximal.

The use of the motorized glider in this study allowed different soaring birds to be tracked, and their progress rate to be accurately calculated, as can be seen from the following table:

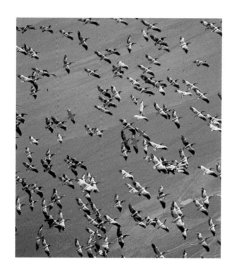

A White Pelican flock migrating - photographed from the motorized glider.
(Photo: Yossi Leshem)

Species	Daily Migration Period (hours)	Average Velocity (kph)	Average Daily Migration Distance (km)
White Pelican	7.5	29.2	249
White Stork	9.0	38.7	348
Lesser Spotted Eagle	7.5	50.9	381
Honey Buzzard	10.0	45.2	446

Pages 168-169:
The motorized glider tracking a flock of storks.
(Photo: Jerry Young)

The data gathered by the motorized glider allowed migration routes to be defined in three dimensions. The horizontal route covered by soaring bird flocks is the aerial distance from the departure point to the arrival point. The surface route covered by migrating flocks is the sum of all horizontal distances measured from thermal to thermal. The three-dimensional route (that includes height) termed the space distance is the sum of the surface route and the vertical route the soaring birds covered from the base of each thermal to its top. Soaring and gliding in thermals significantly extends the distance flocks actually cover. From this data it is possible to estimate by how many kilometers each soaring bird species lengthens its way from breeding to winter quarters. This route extension is made up of several factors: distance added as a result of circumventing the sea and using a longer overland route; distance added due to progress along a surface line from thermal to thermal and not along the shortest aerial line; distance added due to climbing and gliding in thermals.

For example, the center of the Pelican breeding area in Europe is approximately 3885 kilometers away from the presumed center of its winter quarters in Africa; its migration route is extended by 1330 kilometers as a result of flying overland and circumventing the Mediterranean. Flying from thermal to thermal extends its route by an additional 26%. Progress on a space line and use of thermals extend the route by another 31%. As a result of all these the total distance covered by migrating Pelicans can reach 8,200 kilometers! The center of the White Stork breeding area in Europe is approximately 6600 kilometers away from the presumed center of its winter quarters in Africa; its migration route is extended by 1440 kilometers as a result of flying overland and circumventing the Mediterranean. Flying from thermal to thermal extends its route by an additional 26%. Progress on a space line and use of thermals extend the route by another 13%. As a result of all these the total distance covered by migrating White Storks can reach 11,100 kilometers!

The center of the Lesser Spotted Eagle breeding area in Europe is approximately 6500 kilometers away from the presumed center of its winter quarters in Africa; its migration route is extended by 1665 kilometers as a result of flying overland and circumventing the Mediterranean. Flying from thermal to thermal extends its route by an additional 11%. Progress on a space line and use of thermals extend the route by another 12%. As a result of all these the total distance covered by migrating Lesser Spotted Eagles can reach 10,000 kilometers! The center of the Honey Buzzard breeding area in Europe is approximately 8325 kilometers away from the presumed center of its winter quarters in Africa; its migration route is extended by 1920 kilometers as a result of flying overland and circumventing the Mediterranean. Flying from thermal to thermal extends its route by an additional 22%. Progress on a space line and use of thermals extend the route by another 12%. As a result of all these the total distance covered by migrating Honey Buzzards can reach 13,760 kilometers!

A Black Stork on migration.
(Photo: Ofer Bahat)

F. Biological Factors and their Effect on Migrating Birds

The data gathered on migrating soaring birds over Israel shows that seven of the 35 raptor species clearly form large flocks. Other significantly flocking species are the White Stork, Black Stork, Pelican and Crane. Two of the more interesting questions asked about soaring bird migration are: why do some migrate in flocks and what advantage does flocking provide?

As a rule, flock formation in birds has several advantages such as improved ability to spot predators, more efficient food source location, and in communally roosting species, providing an "information center" on food sources. During migration flocking has another major advantage: increased efficiency of thermal location, accompanied by significant energy savings. There is even a theory that claims that flocking improves navigational and orientation ability in migration. This is not very convincing, since in many species juveniles do not migrate with the more experienced adults, but undertake their first migratory journey alone, several weeks after adults have left breeding areas. It would seem, therefore, that the significance of flocking is mainly for locating thermals, thus making the best use of gliding conditions, in order to save as much energy as possible. Soaring birds that fly thousands of kilometers between breeding and winter quarters, must take care to stay on the central migration route and not drift off it. By constantly watching the birds ahead that have already located a thermal and are circling in it, it is easy for a migrating soaring bird to join the route of the flock ahead without wasting time and energy in thermal location. The more flocks there are on a given migration axis, the shorter the individual movements of each flock member both in time and horizontal and vertical distance, compared to migration undertaken by that individual alone.

Migration recorded in the present study by the approach radar at Ben-Gurion International Airport showed that on peak migration days the lines formed by flocks extend to 150 kilometers. Parallel recording from the motorized glider has shown continuous migration lines up to 200 kilometers long. In other words - a continuous air corridor is formed for the individual that allows it to fly on without searching for and locating the migration route. Since the spatial structure of thermals is not uniform, the place occupied by a soaring bird within the thermal is of major importance in determining its most efficient climb rate. This is especially true for weak thermals, when incorrect positioning of the soaring bird can make it abandon the thermal and lose altitude. By watching a flock circling in a thermal the soaring bird can rapidly position itself according to flock movements at an optimal location in the thermal.

Tracking migrating pelicans with the motorized glider has shown that after leaving the thermal and starting to glide they split into dozens of secondary flocks flying in V-formation on an extremely broad front that can extend for a kilometer or more! This allows the pelicans to randomly "sample" air currents, so when part of the flock locates a thermal and begins circling and gaining altitude, the other pelicans immediately begin gliding towards the thermal, and in this manner the flock progresses with optimal efficiency. By this method - the larger a flock, the more efficient it will be in locating thermals and the greater the energy savings for each individual in the flock. This behavior is especially important for pelicans since they migrate in individual flocks over a period of about two months and not within a concentrated interval, as do storks and birds of prey. The latter move in lines dozens of kilometers long and can thus easily locate the next thermal by the behavior of the individuals preceding them.

Comparisons of flocking soaring bird species to non-flocking species show that food type and migration range are related to flocking. Species feeding on poikilothermic (exothermic) prey, such as insects, reptiles, fish and amphibians, migrate completely to Africa, and usually fly south of the Equator, so their migration range is greater than birds feeding on homeothermic (endothermic) prey - mammals and birds. The latter species usually remain partially in Europe or the Mediterranean basin and only rarely fly south of the Equator. Flocking has a distinct advantage for long-distance migrants, since the longer the migration range the more significant the energy savings from flocking. Another major advantage of flocking for insect-eating birds is that the time or place of insect concentrations such as termites or locusts cannot be accurately predicted. The presence of a flock and its spread over a given area significantly increase the chances of locating this type of food.

Another very interesting facet of soaring bird migration has been found from comparison of average arrival times in spring and autumn of different species. It seems the major food type each species feeds on has a decisive effect on its arrival in Israel during migration, or in other words on its passage time from breeding to winter quarters and back. A major part of the diet of soaring birds such as the Honey Buzzard and the White Stork is composed of insects, and they are the first to leave their breeding areas in Europe and Asia in autumn and migrate south. They are followed by species feeding mainly on reptiles, such as the Short-toed Eagle or those feeding on a variety of food that includes insects, amphibians, reptiles, birds and mammals, such as the Levant Sparrowhawk and the Black Kite. After them migrate species feeding on mammals and a combination of insects, reptiles and amphibians, such as the Lesser Spotted Eagle and the Red-footed Falcon. These are followed by fish-eaters (pelicans) and finally by the Steppe Eagle that feeds mainly on mammals and carrion in its breeding quarters. The relation between preferred food to migration time is mainly a result of seasonal changes in weather, principally the decrease in

Red-footed Falcon on migration.
(Photo: Noah Satat)

A day in the migration of a pelican flock over Israel

A pelican flock lands in the late afternoon in the Hula Nature Reserve to spend the night.
(Upper photo: Yig'al Livneh)

The ground-based observers locate the flock and report its location. In the morning the motorized glider arrives
and awaits patiently, outside the reserve, until the pelicans take off (usually between 8:30-9:15 A.M.).
(Lower photo, from the motorized glider: Duby Tal, Albatross Inc.)

The motorized glider joins the pelican flock immediately after it takes off and flies besides it, wing to wing, during the migration day, for about ten and a half continuous hours.
(Upper photo: Ofer Bahat)

After gliding over the city of Safed and the Meron Mountains, the pelican flock crosses the Jezreel Valley and glides in several V-formations across the wooded Carmel hills.
(Lower photo, from the motorized glider: Yossi Leshem)

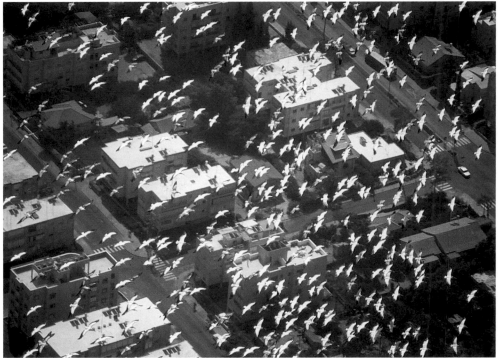

The pelican flock continues south above the citrus groves on the Coastal Plain. The well-coordinated turns of the pelicans in the flock can be clearly seen from the glider.
(Upper photo, from the motorized glider: Yossi Leshem)

Towards noon, the flock flies at low altitude over the city of Petah-Tiqva, where most of the inhabitants have no idea of what goes on above their heads.
(Lower photo, from the motorized glider: Yossi Leshem)

During the early afternoon the pelican flock reaches the Gaza Strip. At this point gliding conditions deteriorate, the pelicans lose altitude, having to beat their wings at times in order to remain aloft.
(Upper photo, from the motorized glider: Ofer Bahat)

In the late afternoon the pelicans did not find a good landing site in densely populated Gaza, so they turn into the Mediterranean opposite Rafiah, where they land for the night, about seven kilometers from the coast. The pelican flock flew over three major Israel Air Force bases during this day. The motorized glider and the "bird center" at Ben-Gurion International Airport provided real-time warnings on the flock location thus preventing the danger of collisions with air force planes.
(Lower photo: Ron Be'er)

temperatures in autumn. The first animals to disappear with the onset of cold weather are insects, followed by reptiles and then amphibians. Later in the season, as water bodies freeze, fish too become unavailable to predators. At this stage most of the birds breeding in the north have already migrated south. Finally mammals disappear, some hibernating, while others spend most of their time in burrows or sheltered sites and are unavailable to raptors. During spring, when birds migrate back to their breeding quarters the situation is reversed. The Steppe Eagle that feeds on mammals, is the first to migrate north, passing over Israel from mid-February, while the Honey Buzzard that feeds mainly on insects flies over last, closing the spring migratory season in Israel in the beginning of May! When these two "extreme" species are compared, it can be seen that the Honey Buzzard spends a mere three months in its breeding quarters, since it is forced to leave the area in mid-August, returning again only at the end of May, when insect activity is full renewed. The Steppe Eagle on the other hand, leaves its breeding quarters only in mid-October when small mammals cease activity and returns as early as the last week in March, thus spending about seven months in its breeding quarters.

Analysis of soaring bird passage times over Israel brings to light another fascinating fact: the passage period of all raptor species is shorter in autumn (47-64 days) than in spring (36-102 days). When flocking and non-flocking species are compared, the passage period of all flocking species is shorter than that of non-flocking species, both in autumn and in spring. Ninety percent of the flocking species pass over in autumn during 13-20 days, compared to 24-35 days for non-flocking species. In spring 90% of the flocking species pass over within 9-33 days, compared to 39-62 days in non-flocking species. Similar findings were found for the White Stork too: in autumn 90% of the population pass over during 28 days compared to 43 days in spring. In addition, the stronger the tendency a species exhibits for flocking, the greater the proportion of birds flying over during peak migration days, reaching 24% in autumn and 46% in spring! In non-flocking species, the number of individuals flying over on peak migration days is relatively smaller, reaching 16% in autumn and 12% in spring. Analysis of these data shows the following:

The larger the breeding quarter area of a given flocking soaring bird species, the longer its passage period over Israel, and inversely: the smaller the breeding quarter areas of the species, the shorter its passage time over Israel. Some birds of prey winter in very small areas in Africa where they feed on insects. One such case is the Levant Sparrowhawk that migrates in large flocks that can include thousands of individuals, during an extremely short time: in spring, when it returns from Africa, its population passes over Israel in nine days as opposed to 13 in autumn. On the peak migration day in spring 46% of the population passes over, compared to 17% in autumn! In soaring birds that reach sexual maturity only after several years, there is a statistically significant difference in passage times of adults compared to those of immatures. Steppe Eagles for example, reach sexual maturity at the age of four or five years. Only adults, hurrying to return to their breeding grounds and occupy territories, pass over in the beginning of February in spring. Juveniles and immatures pass over only later in spring, mainly in April. The White Stork exhibits similar behavior: in spring adults begin passing over in February, while immatures migrate only in April and May. In autumn the process is reversed: first come the tremendous migratory waves of immatures, during the first three weeks in August, followed only later adults flying to their winter quarters in Africa.

Pelicans are exceptional compared to other soaring birds. Despite the fact that they flock, their migratory wave is the longest, continuing for 114 days in autumn! In spring their migration is lengthy as well - from the beginning of March until the end of May! Pelicans flock while breeding and wintering and not only during migration, in other words they are totally dependent on flock structure. The pelican breeding range, unlike that of other soaring birds, is not continuous but limited to several colonies on river deltas and lake shores over a broad geographic range - from Greece in the west to the Balchas Sea in Russia in the east. This seems to be the reason for their unusual migratory pattern. Pelican flocks, originating in different sites, sometimes very far apart, apparently begin migrating at the same time. Thus, Pelicans breeding in Turkey or Romania probably are the first to fly over Israel on their way south. Pelicans originating in distant breeding grounds such as the Ural Sea, apparently fly over later.

A Honey Buzzard feeding its young in the nest.
(Photo: Jose Luis Gonzalez, Bruce Coleman Limited)

Page 178:
The entire global population of the Levant Sparrowhawk passes over Israel during spring and autumn migration.
(Photo: Ofer Bahat)

G. Weather Effects on Soaring Bird Migration.

This study found migration times, magnitude, routes and altitude to be closely linked to climatic conditions. This relation is so distinct that weather data can even allow the prediction of changes in the character of migration.

Weather can affect migration on a broad scale and on a local scale. Global climatic changes in breeding and wintering quarters and along the migration route affect the character of soaring bird migration in time and space. Cold air from Europe encounters warm air from Africa over the Mediterranean and this meeting enhances synoptic systems. Changes in synoptic conditions - temperature, relative humidity, pressure and wind - create conditions that affect soaring bird migration over hundreds and even thousands of kilometers. This phenomenon was observed mainly in autumn, when the low barometric pressure area from the north triggers the birds departure. Passage of cold fronts is beneficial to soaring birds since it produces northwesterly winds that create appropriate conditions for air currents to rise along mountain ranges. In spring, warm southwesterly winds apparently contribute to the strong movement of birds of prey. Local climatic factors have weaker and shorter effects on migration.

Climatic factors significantly affecting soaring bird migratory behavior include:

Wind direction and strength - Wind direction and strength determine the ground velocity of the bird's progress. A soaring bird flying at a given aerial speed is deflected from its migration route according to the direction and strength of the wind. The bird usually "corrects" its direction so that actually it moves along its "planned" route, as long as it maintains a constant progress angle relative to wind direction. In a given area wind is affected by topography, local climate and turbulence caused by the ground heating, so that migrating birds, at a given site and time, encounter winds whose direction and strength vary.

Vertical wind flow - soaring birds are affected by two main types of upcurrents: thermals - heat conducted to the atmosphere as a result of the ground warming up and horizontal air currents deflected upwards as a result of hitting mountains, cliffs, trees and other objects. Although birds exploit both types of rising air currents, the former plays a major role in migration. A thermal is formed after the sun's rays warm the ground, causing the air in contact with it to warm up. The heat and pressure gradient formed cause the warm air to rise, while cold air from below replaces it and an air bubble that rises is formed. Air flowing on the bubble surface creates internal turbulence and circular spinning and further heating causes the warm air bubble to continue rising and additional cold air from below to penetrate. The soaring birds circle on the warm turbulence in the bubble, rising with it until the bubble dissolves. According to another explanation, warm air is found not only in the bubble in the thermal's upper portion, but flows continuously, rising from the ground to the top of the thermal. Thermals apparently "breathe" and constantly change, so that both descriptions are partially correct and blend with each other.

The mass of warm air in the thermal usually rises to an altitude of about 1.5 kilometers and sometimes even higher. The intensity of the thermal is dependent on various factors such as the character of the surface and its reflection, the direction it faces (principally if north or south), strength of the horizontal wind, magnitude of the temperature gradient with the rise in altitude, cloud cover and geographic location. Strong thermals usually develop three to five hours after sunrise.

Studies done in the United States using radar found that the average rate of thermal development between 6:35 and 10:20 A.M., was 228 meters per hour (3.8 meters a minute) and that the thermal reached an altitude of 1000 meters above the ground. In another case the thermal rate of rise between 7:00 and 8:00 A.M. was 2 meters a minute, growing to 6.1 meters a minute between 10:00 and 11:30 A.M., reaching an altitude of 1600 meters above the ground. Thermal diameter grows as the air warms up and was found to be between 100 and 200 meters up to 9:00 A.M., increasing to 1000 meters towards noon.

Other factors affecting soaring bird migration are barometric pressure, temperature and relative humidity. Their effect however, is not always distinct, since they affect

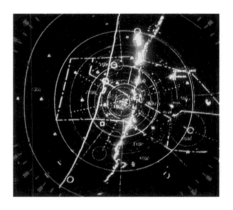

Honey Buzzards on a regular migration day, migrating on a narrow front several hundred meters wide.

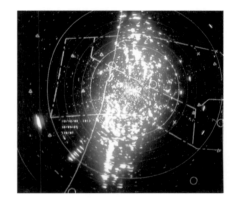

On 19 September 1989 strong easterly winds spread the migration front to a width of 23 kilometers.

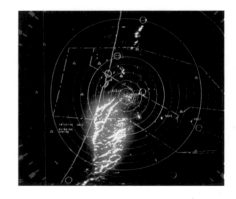

On 24 March 1989 20 knot-strong southeasterly winds were recorded at an azimuth of 120 degrees. A giant 35,000-stork flock drifted towards the coast, west of its usual migration route. The storks progressed to the northeast in order to correct the westerly drift and return to their original route. The width of their progress front reached approximately 16 kilometers.

other factors related to migration, such as the direction and strength of winds and thermal formation. Rain, cloudiness and limited visibility, unlike the previous factors, significantly affect soaring bird migration. Soaring birds fly very little on rainy days and usually cease migrating. Dense cloud cover and poor visibility significantly also reduce migration magnitude. These circumstances create unsuitable soaring conditions and make locating landmarks difficult due to poor visibility.

In the present study weather data was collected in the field and data from the meteorological service was analyzed. During motorized glider flights wind direction and velocity were recorded hourly according to information transmitted from the control tower closest to the glider (usually Israel Air Force base control towers). At the same time weather conditions as seen from the glider were recorded every two hours, including cloud type, percentage of cloud cover and the cloud base altitude. Other weather phenomena such as rain, haze and fog were recorded as well. Meteorological data gathered in the field were processed with data from the meteorological service in order to examine their effect on soaring bird migration. The data was analyzed from several major aspects: appearance time of various migrant species, the number of individuals flying over, horizontal and vertical migration routes, and daily, seasonal and annual migration axis movements.

Analysis of passage dates of soaring birds on a yearly scale shows that first appearance dates are highly accurate. In some soaring bird species average appearance days were found to vary within a range of only one to three days during nine consecutive tracking years! Since the birds time their migration dates according to changes in day length, the major factor affecting variance in migration timing is weather. Following are several cases illustrating this fact: The last week in September or the first week in October is usually the peak week for Lesser Spotted Eagle migration over Israel in autumn. In 1986 a drastic reduction in the number of migrating eagles during the first three days in October was recorded. When comparing data from autumn 1986 and 1985, we find that in 1985 there was a sharp rise in the number of Lesser Spotted Eagles during the first days of October, whereas in 1986 on those same days there was a sharp decrease in their numbers.

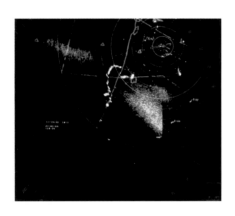

On 23 March 1989, at 11:19 A.M., a stork flock was seen about 3.5 kilometers west of the Mediterranean coastline, opposite Palmahim. Wind strength was 25 knots and blew at an azimuth of 120 degrees. A triangle (probably haze) can be seen southeast of the stork flock, that was deflected to a distance of about 30 kilometers over the sea by the wind.
(Photo of the Ben-Gurion International Airport radar screen: Yossi Leshem)

Lesser Spotted Eagle numbers counted in autumn 1985 and 1986

Year / Date	27/9	28/9	29/9	30/9	1/10	2/10	3/10
1985	7006	11133	4716	8301	2877	7373	24767
1986	17859	15584	26553	12553	187	160	3407

Meteorological data gathered in autumn 1986 from Europe and the Mediterranean basin show a barometric depression moving from Russia towards our area. It caused a delay in migration, as illustrated clearly in satellite photos: in a photo from 29 September 1986, a barometric depression can be seen over Russia, northern Turkey, Greece and Italy. The skies of central and southern Turkey, as well as of the entire Middle East are clear, providing optimal migration conditions and accordingly 26,553 Lesser Spotted Eagles were counted over Israel. Three days later, on 2 October 1986, the depression can be In a satellite photo seen after it moved south, covering Turkey, Lebanon and Israel. Heavy rains, strong winds and dense clouds caused migration to come to a standstill. On that same day, 2.10.1986, the approach radar screen at Ben-Gurion International Airport showed dense, heavy clouds and a total absence of birds! The strong winds and rains, stopped the Lesser Spotted Eagles flying south from migrating further. They were forced to wait until the depression passed on 3 October 1986. Between 4 and 8 October 1986, 22,151 Lesser Spotted Eagles were counted flying over Israel (as opposed to 11,151 on the same date in 1985). The many eagles that passed over during these dates in autumn 1986 were the same eagles that had been delayed as a result of the barometric depression along their migration route between Turkey, Lebanon and Israel.

A Lesser Spotted Eagle on the tree in Ben-Shemen Forest where it roosted, before flying off on migration.
(Photo: Ofer Bahat)

Another example of the effect weather conditions have on migration occurred in autumn 1986 during the migration of Red-footed Falcons. This raptor is one of the "sea crossing" species and Israel is located on the eastern periphery of its migration

A Lesser Spotted Eagle on migration - photographed from the motorized glider.
(Photo: Yossi Leshem)

A White Stork on migration.
(Photo: Pierre Perin)

route. In view of its ability to migrate over sea, part of this species' population crosses the Mediterranean during autumn migration and only a tiny percentage passes over the coastal plain in Israel. In autumn 1986 a total of 4481 Red-footed Falcons, comprising approximately 80% of the total population counted that season, passed over during three days between 3 and 5 October. Meteorological data showed, that the same barometric depression that had affected the Lesser Spotted Eagle migration, caused strong westerly winds, deflecting the Red-footed Falcons from their usual migration route over the Mediterranean into the coastal plain. These falcons had to stop migrating due to the tempestuous weather, but continued south once the depression had passed. During the Honey Buzzard migration wave in autumn 1982 migration was delayed by tempestuous weather and followed by a "flood" of migrants. On 10 September 1982, 117,636 Honey Buzzards passed over in one day followed by another 124,041 the next day. During these two days, a total of 241,676 Honey Buzzards was counted, consisting of about 75% of the total population of this species migrating over Israel in autumn 1982. This occurrence was unequaled during the nine years of the study. An active weather system including heavy rain in the area between the Caspian Sea and eastern Turkey, caused Honey Buzzard migration to cease completely in the area. Between 7 and 8 September 1982 there was a break in the bad weather that allowed the Honey Buzzards that had concentrated in the area to continue migrating and they passed over Israel on 10 and 11 September 1982.

Weather conditions have a significant effect in spring as well as in autumn. One such case was the unusual Steppe Eagle migration in spring 1985, when 75,063 Steppe Eagles were counted over the Eilat Mountains, 2.6 times more than the annual average (28,134 eagles). Most of the Steppe Eagles passed over between 5 and 9 March 1985, dates on which in previous years only several hundred eagles had been counted. This unusual migration was caused by the development of an unusually lengthy Red Sea Trough between 3 and 19 March 1985 up to an altitude of 1600 meters that included strong southeasterly winds in the Red Sea as well as dense cloud development over the northern Red Sea. These unusual weather conditions deflected the Steppe Eagles off their regular course in Sinai, north towards the Eilat Mountains, unlike the situation in normal weather conditions.

In spring 1985 only 905 Levant Sparrowhawks passed over the Eilat area, as opposed to the annual average of 16,278 usually counted in the area. When weather conditions for the usual dates this species migrates over Eilat were examined, two unusual incidents were found to have occurred between 21 and 26 April 1985. There were strong winds and sandstorms in the area between Egypt and Saudi Arabia and from 24 April there was also a strong, warm barometric depression over the Nile Delta with strong winds and sandstorms in Egypt and Sinai. The Levant Sparrowhawks could not continue migrating under these conditions, and apparently circumvented the tempestuous area from the east via the Arabian Peninsula and Jordan. Another case involving Levant Sparrowhawks occurred in spring 1987 when a total of 49,386 individuals passed over, three times the annual average. A lengthy (9 days) barometric depression was seen over Saudi Arabia, the air was saturated with sand, and strong winds blew on 25 and 26 April 1987. The weather conditions resulting from the depression apparently deflected the Levant Sparrowhawks from their usual migratory route so that the major part of their global population passed over the Eilat Mountains.

In addition to the influence of weather on passage times and migration routes, local weather conditions also have a significant effect on migration, expressed mainly as variations in progress rate and daily distances covered. One such case took place during a tracking flight with a Pelican flock on 2 November 1986. The 500-bird flock roosted in the Hula Nature Reserve. Most Pelican flocks roosting in the reserve fly off between 8:30 and 9:15 A.M. On the date in question the weather was cloudy and rainy and the cloud base was 500 meters above the ground. The first 96 Pelicans attempted to fly off at 9:40. For 15 minutes they tried to gain altitude, failed and landed again. At 10:10 the flock took off and flew heavily along the Naftali Mountains west of the reserve, due south. By 11:15 they had covered only 15 kilometers compared to the usual 35-70 kilometers on similar days, when flying conditions are better. Strong easterly and southeasterly winds accompanied by hot, dry weather tend to deflect the migration axis to the west. On 23 March 1989 strong easterly winds, with speeds between 15 and 30 knots (27-54 kilometers per hour), deflected

Pages 184-185:
A flock of White Pelicans flying off on migration along Israel's Mediterranean coast.
(Photo: Yig'al Livneh)

On 29 September 1986 clear skies can be seen over Israel and Jordan in this satellite photo. Migration was accordingly strong on this day.

On 2 October 1986 a barometric depression appeared over our area. The heavy rains and clouds completely stopped migration.

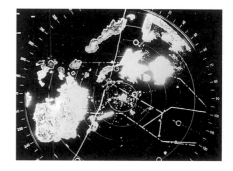

This photo of the radar screen at Ben-Gurion International Airport, taken at the same time as the satellite photo on 2 October 1986, confirms data from the ground observers. Only rain clouds can be seen on the screen, and not a single migrating flock.
(Radar screen photo: Pini Magor)

183

White Storks from their original migration axis west into the sea. With the help of the motorized glider and the approach radar at Ben-Gurion International Airport the storks were tracked and located as far out as 7 kilometers into the sea. At 9:54 A.M. the glider joined a flock of about 2000 storks flying in a combination of flapping flight and gliding 5.4 kilometers west of the coast opposite Ashdod, at an average altitude of 330 meters above the sea. Radar photos from that day showed clearly that the storks that had been swept over the sea tried to correct their route by zig-zagging towards the coastline. The hot weather broke the next day at noon and the wind became west northwesterly. The radar screen photos showed that the storks had returned to their usual migration route and behavior.

Soaring bird migration routes drift as a result of strong easterly winds in autumn too, as recorded on one of the motorized glider flights with a flock of Pelicans on 16 October 1987, a day with strong easterly winds. Close to 2000 Pelicans took off at 8:50 A.M. from the Hula Nature Reserve on their way south. They immediately rose on a thermal with the help of strong gusts blowing towards the Naftali Mountains and soared upwards. Within five minutes they had reached an altitude of 660 meters and 30 minutes after flying off they had reached an altitude of 1500 meters. In normal weather conditions this can take between an hour and an hour and a half! Because of the strong easterly winds the Pelicans did not progress along their usual route but drifted rapidly west. After about an hour and 45 minutes they landed in the Zebulun Valley near the Mediterranean coast.

Weather conditions also affect two additional factors: migration speed and altitude. This can be seen from two motorized glider flights tracking Honey Buzzards, the first on 1 September 1986 and the second on 4 September 1986. The Honey Buzzards flew on two similar, completely parallel routes on these days. Weather conditions were identical on the two days with one exception: wind strength. On the first day the wind blew with a force of 10-13 knots (18-24 kilometers per hour), while on the second its force was a mere 0-5 knots (0-9 kilometers per hour). When flight altitude was examined migration on 1 September was found to be at a higher altitude and at an average velocity of 48 kilometers per hour, as opposed to 42 kilometers per hour on 4 September. These data show that wind speed higher by an average of 9 knots (16 kilometers per hour) increased migration flight velocity by an average 12.5%! On a day like this, the Honey Buzzards would be able to fly about 60 additional kilometers.

A Honey Buzzard resting during migration in the Eilat Mountain area. (Photo: Paul Doherty)

Motorized glider tracking flights with Honey Buzzards over the Eilat Mountains showed that changes in wind regime significantly affect not only migration speed but its altitude as well. Between 5 and 10 May 1987 Honey Buzzard migration was tracked in the Eilat Mountains. On 5 May severe heat wave developed in the area and instead of the usual northerly winds, strong southerly winds blew, which prevented thermal formation, stopping Honey Buzzard migration completely. Towards 8 May the heat broke and northerly and northwesterly winds began blowing, renewing the flow of Honey Buzzards. Whereas on 7 May only 55 Honey Buzzards were counted, on 8 May 19,992 flew over, on 9 May 70,987 and on 10 May 32,762. Data from several representative days showed that on 5 May at the peak of the heat wave, the Honey Buzzards flew at low altitudes, close to the ground, at an average speed of only 19 kilometers per hour. On 8 May, when the heat broke, the upper thermal layer of Honey Buzzards rose to 820 meters above ground, and their average progress rate increased to 36 kilometers per hour. On 10 May soaring conditions were perfect and the Honey Buzzards soared in thermals up to an average altitude of 1565 meters and their average progress rate rose to 46 kilometers per hour.

Alterations in flight route and altitude can be caused by sudden changes in weather, but sometimes this change is beneficial and soaring birds passing from one area to another can exploit good weather conditions that permit improved gliding. On a tracking flight with a White Stork flock flying on the western route, on 3 April 1988, weather conditions were bad and the storks were unable to fly at altitudes higher than 200-250 meters and at average speeds of 28.7 kilometers per hour (34% lower than the annual average). In the Bet Shemesh area the storks turned northeast, east of the central mountain range watershed, where cumulus clouds developed at an altitude of 8000 feet and soaring conditions were excellent. The result was immediately obvious: the storks' flight altitude rose to 1,550 meters and their flight speed doubled to 56.9 kilometers per hour. Within 72 minutes the storks succeeded in crossing all of Samaria on two particularly long glides, the first 36 kilometers long and the second 19 kilometers long.

On 22 September 1987, the motorized glider followed Black Storks along the eastern route over the Jordan Valley. As a result of bad soaring conditions the storks flew off only at 9:40 A.M. (one hour later than usual) and progressed at a low altitude at a velocity between only 28 and 36 kilometers per hour. After four hours they left the Jordan valley axis and flew west towards the eastern slopes of the Judean and Hebron Mountains. The improved soaring conditions enabled the storks to rise to an altitude of 1500 meters above the ground within a short period of time and increase their progress speed to 52 kilometers per hour.

H. The Bird Plagued Zone (BPZ) Map

The main purpose of this study was to provide the Israel Air Force with data that would help prevent bird-aircraft collisions. As early as the end of the first year of the study, maps with details of the major migration routes were plotted. Low-altitude flight was forbidden in these areas and procedures were formulated for flight plans during migration and what to do in case of birdstrike. The Israel Air Force coined a new expression - Bird Plagued Zone - based on the MPZ (Missile Plagued Zone) and distributed maps to the pilots were named BPZ maps.

The motorized glider following a flock of Black Storks and Steppe Buzzards. (Drawing: James P. Smith)

187

BPZ maps were updated yearly according to new data gathered in this study. When the study was completed a final version of BPZ maps for spring and autumn was distributed to all flight squadrons in the Israel Air Force, with compulsory regulations for the entire fighter aircraft network. Altitude is a major factor in these maps, since during the study most soaring birds were found to migrate at an altitude between 0 and 1000 meters above the ground. Since BPZ procedures close significant portions of Israeli air space to air force planes during migration, opening and closing times were determined for BPZ routes according to migration timing as determined by the study. In this manner the fighter aircraft could make maximal use of the days available for training, without endangering pilot lives.

One operative result of the study in the Israel Air Force was the establishment of a "bird center" that links flight control units, the Israel Air Force Central Command and its bases. It was set up at one of the radar consoles at Ben-Gurion International Airport, in order to provide real-time information on migrating flocks. For seven months out of every year, four air force radar operators man the "bird center", and an Israel Air Force flight controller (a reserve officer or a biologist) supervises the operation of the entire system. All information on bird movements in Israeli air space is immediately passed on to the relevant air force bases. In this manner, each base knows when migrating birds are approaching and can prepare itself accordingly, mainly by warning aircraft in the air and avoiding low-altitude flights while birds are flying over the base. Take-off and landing procedures are also modified according to the presence of birds in the area.

In order to improve the real-time warning system, as well as to allow aircraft to fly during BPZ periods or on low-density migration days when the danger of collision is minimal, the ground observers were also connected to the "bird center". During the study it became apparent that on 35-45% of all migration days the number of migrating birds is very small, so that low-altitude flights with minimal risk are possible. In view of this, a procedure was developed, that allowed aircraft to fly at low altitudes within BPZ zones during migration, conditional to ground observers and radar locating only slight migration. In these cases, the information is passed on to the "bird center" and low-altitude flights are approved. If a migrating flock is seen, the center is immediately warned to put BPZ regulations into effect again. This unique procedure allowed the Israel Air Force to continue flying at low altitudes during a third of BPZ days with minimal risk and no collisions.

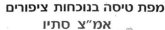

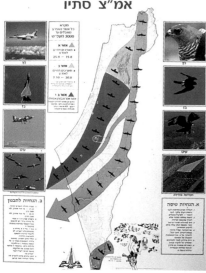

The study results were applied to prepare a BPZ (Bird Plagued Zone) map for Israel Air Force fighter aircraft, which determines when, where and at which altitude flight is forbidden during the migration seasons.
(Courtesy of the Israel Air Force)

I. The Significant Reduction of Bird-Aircraft Collisions

In order to increase the awareness of Israel Air Force pilots to BPZ regulations, a campaign named "Take Care - We Share the Air" was organized. Every year colorful posters, video-tapes and stickers were distributed among the flight squadrons. Lectures on the subject were given with slides and films, and a photo exhibit shown at the various air force bases. This widespread "marketing" campaign showed immediate results. The increased awareness and new procedures brought about a significant reduction in bird-aircraft collisions in the Israel Air Force. Comparison of birdstrike data before and after BPZ regulations went into effect shows the following situation:

Birdstrike led to the loss of three pilots and eight fighter aircraft between 1970 and 1998. During the years before this study dozens of serious collisions occurred, causing severe damage to planes amounting to more than one-half a million dollars per collision. In the fourteen years following the instatement of BPZ regulations serious collisions decreased by 76%.

Hundreds of accidents involving migrating birds and aircraft resulting in minor damage (up to 20,000 dollars per collision) occurred between 1970 and 1984. Minor damage collisions decreased by 81% since BPZ procedures were put into effect! In the years since BPZ procedures were formulated the Israel Air Force has had to learn to maneuver in extremely limited air space that includes the major soaring bird

The threatening appearance of a "hawk" (F-16) fighter plane over the Negev.
(Photo: Gil Arbel, Israel Air Force Magazine)

Pages 190-191:
Posters produced jointly by the Israel Air Force and the Society for the Protection of Nature in Israel in order to increase pilot
awareness to the dangers posed by migrating birds and to the importance of flying according to BPZ regulations.
(Courtesy of the Israel Air Force)

A male Levant Sparrowhawk resting during migration in the Eilat Mountains.
(Photo: Hadoram Shirihai)

migration routes (since 1982, when Sinai was returned to Egypt as part of the peace agreements). It is reasonable to assume that without these procedures the proportion of damages would be many times greater. In addition, damage in the past (before BPZ regulations) was to older planes such as Mirages and Skyhawks, worth only a few million dollars each. The new generation of planes in the Israel Air Force is vastly more expensive: An F-16 fighter plane costs about 27 million dollars (unarmed), while the cost of an F-15 can reach 50 million dollars! The IAF calculated that damages caused by soaring birds could have reached an annual value of 30 million dollars without BPZ regulations. In other words this study has saved the IAF 450 million dollars during the period between 1984 when it started and the present!

The Israel Air Force has lately purchased F-15I fighter aircraft, valued at 86 million dollars per plane, which means that the cost of damage caused to aircraft by birdstrike would double. The success of this joint study by the Israel Air Force, the Society for the Protection of Nature in Israel, Tel-Aviv University and the Ministry of Science was unparalleled: even the air force pilots were skeptical at the start about the possibility of reducing damage by migrating birds so significantly. The joint research project succeeded in attaining peaceful coexistence between fighter aircraft and migrating birds despite Israel's unique position on the migratory map of the world.

The results of the study have been presented at several international conferences and have become a worldwide success story, attracting representatives of western air forces who come to learn the Israel Air Force procedures on the subject.

In January 1992 the Israel Air Force, the Society for the Protection of Nature in Israel and Tel-Aviv University established the "Feather Remains Identification Laboratory". Judy Shamoun-Baranes from Tel-Aviv University is preparing a detailed catalog of feather remains, with the help of light and electronic microscopes, under the supervision of Professor Yoram Yom-Tov. The purpose of this catalog is to allow a bird species to be identified according to the unique structure of its feathers (a sort of "fingerprint" catalog of birds found in Israel). This center will make it possible to accurately identify the species of birds involved in collisions with aircraft in the future and to anticipate the approach to the problem according to the species involved. In a cooperative venture with the Royal Netherland Air Force (RNAF), Amsterdam University, the Expert Center for Taxonomic Identification (ETI), IAF, SPNI and Tel-Aviv University, Judy Shimoun-Baranes and Wilhlmin Prust prepared BRIS - the Bird Remains Identification System - on a CD-Rom. This system allows about 200 species of birds to be identified from remains collected after collisions.

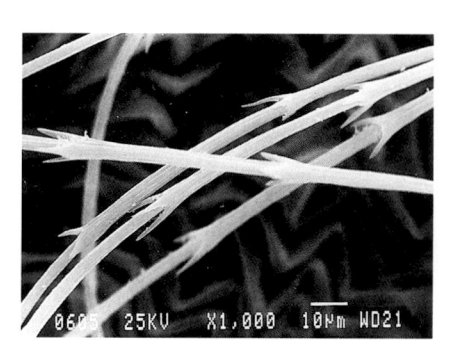

This scanning electron microscope photo of a Long-eared Owl feather enlarged 1000 times was prepared at the Feather Remains Identification Laboratory run jointly by the Israel Air Force, the Society for the Protection of Nature in Israel and Tel-Aviv University, in cooperation with the Royal Netherland Air Force and Amsterdam University, ETI.
(Photo: Professor Tsvi Malik)

Judy Shamoun-Baranes, who is in charge of the Feather Remains Identification Laboratory, examining the remains of a feather with the help of a computer program developed jointly with Holland. (Photo: Lior Rubin)

J. The Effect of Migration on Birdwatching in Israel

Research results have shown that Israel is one of the best, if not the best place in the world to watch soaring bird migration. This fact is recognized internationally more and more, and has led to several international congresses on migration in Israel.

The many popular publications on the subject in the media have put Israel on the international birdwatching map. Eilat and its surroundings are a major attraction for birdwatchers coming to Israel from all over the world. The International Birdwatching Center in Eilat was established jointly by several tourism factors in Israel. The center has developed a special birdwatching trail adjacent to the Eilat salt pans, which an estimated 10,000 birdwatchers from all over the world visit annually (compared to a few dozen in the past). Tens of thousands of nature lovers, school classes, soldiers and the public at large have visited the migration surveys organized by the Society for the Protection of Nature in Israel in Samaria (the Kfar Qasem survey) and later in the northern valleys. The public is fascinated by the uniqueness of bird migration over Israel and the millions of migrating birds converging over the area. This has led to formation of a direct connection to nature and increased awareness of the public at large to the subject of nature conservation in Israel. For many people these surveys have provided the first opportunity to watch a migrating stork or eagle and to enjoy the fantastic phenomenon of bird migration.

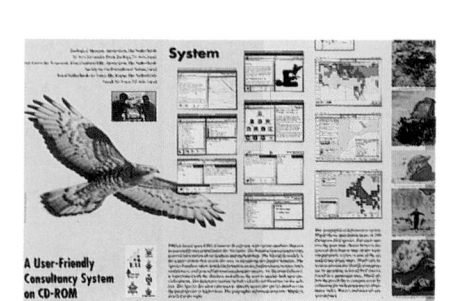

The CD-ROM with 200 common birds from Europe and the Middle East mapped allows relatively rapid identification of feather remains in case of accidents.

Page 194:
A flock of storks migrating over the Negev desert.
(Drawing: James P. Smith)

193

Chapter 6

How to Watch Migrating Birds in Israel

לְמֵרָחוֹק עֵינָיו יַבִּיטוּ (איוב ל״ט, כט)

"Her eyes behold it afar off."
(Job, 39:29)

A. Birdwatching

Although an estimated 500 million birds migrate twice a year in the skies of Israel, most people know only a few of them and are unaware that only a short drive from almost anyplace in the country they can watch this unique natural phenomenon. All that you need is some basic information, inquisitive eyes and a pair of binoculars (or if possible, a telescope). Binoculars magnify at least seven times and a magnification of ten times is best for birdwatching. For birds farther away a telescope, with a magnification of 20 or more, is your best bet. The gulls inhabiting the seashore and fields, the Pied Wagtails visiting gardens, streets and open spaces and the Black Kites feeding on garbage in dumps seen regularly over the Coastal Highway are a common sight in Israel. All these are migrants coming to Israel from their breeding quarters in the north to spend the winter. Nevertheless, millions of passerines and water birds migrating over Israel on their way to Africa do so mainly at night, and can best be seen during the day when they stop to rest and feed.

Migration can be watched close to home and all you need is a site that can be visited regularly to watch the species inhabiting it change with the seasons. Such a spot can be the view from the window, the house garden or yard, an open field or nearby park, or any location that is easily reached. Obviously, a smaller variety of species will be seen in a dense urban environment, but the further out one wanders, to open habitats where birds find food and rest, the larger the number of species that can be seen. The easiest birds to see are the common migrants that herald the coming of autumn or spring and the start of migration, or those species that come to spend the winter or summer in Israel such as the Pied Wagtail, Stonechat, Starling, Swift, Barn Swallow, Chaffinch, Chiffchaff and many more. If you would like to make birdwatching your hobby, possibilities are endless: record the number of individuals seen in the observation area, species composition and how it varies throughout the year, and of course additional details on the bird's behavior, food or any other interesting detail. You should also have a bird guide and notebook or diary for recording information in addition to binoculars. Some guides have drawings of the birds, while others have photographs. Any guide is helpful for identification, but should also have information on range, the bird's status in Israel (whether the bird is resident, wintering, a passage migrant, etc.), as well as information on specific identifying marks, such as color differences between sexes, calls and so on. The best way to watch birds is in pairs or small groups, which facilitates watching the bird while recording pertinent information. Another set of eyes usually increases the probability of finding birds as well.

Recording changes in the numbers of resident species throughout the year in a chosen observation can be very interesting, since sometimes a migrant population will join a resident population of the same species, as is the case in Kestrels, Cattle Egrets, Spur-winged Plovers and other birds. Another important detail concerns the identification of a rare species or an unusual plumage in a common species. Sometimes while birdwatching, a bird with unusual plumage will be seen, or one whose identification is uncertain or is very rare or even new to Israel (not listed as appearing in Israel in the guide, or listed as appearing during a different season). In these cases it is important to record a detailed description of the bird's appearance and coloring and if possible to photograph it as well. The identification should be confirmed by consulting with experienced birdwatchers or ornithological organizations who can help, such as the SPNI's Ornithology Center.

A White Stork on a roosting tree at sunset.
(Photo: Paul Doherty)

Page 196:
A Spoonbill reflected in a pond.
(Photo: Noah Satat)

Page 199:
A Sparrowhawk feeding on its prey
(photographed in England).
(Photo: John Hawkins, FLPA)

When watching birds do not approach them too closely or make noise, so as not to disturb or frighten them. Disturbances are particularly harmful to migrating birds that face enough dangers and difficulties during migration as is. Try not to face the sun, to avoid being blinded by the light and also because in these conditions it is very difficult to see and distinguish the colors and shades so vital for identifying the birds. In open areas it is wise to watch birds from a vehicle to reduce the probability of frightening them, and to be able to approach them closer than would be possible on foot. Walking up to the bank of a water reservoir, for example, can frighten ducks and other water birds and make them scatter. The best way is to approach the observation point slowly and not appear suddenly at sites where birds are. Do not walk openly towards birds, but parallel to them, approaching gradually. In many cases it is preferable to sit in one place near where birds gather, such as a field they feed in, rather than walk around. Birds usually become accustomed to the presence of an observer who sits quietly and will continue their normal behavior and sometimes even approach the birdwatcher. Any behavioral sign of suspicion, such as warning calls, nervous movements or moving away from the observer, should be taken as a clear warning sign to immediately cease approaching the birds.

Weather affects bird migration considerably, so it should be taken into account when planning a birdwatching expedition. Tempestuous, rainy days are usually not suitable, except for watching water birds that fly near the seashore and can be seen more than usual on such days. Clear days following stormy ones are usually excellent for watching migration, since many birds stop migrating in bad weather, but come out again when it clears to continue migrating or engage in other activities such as feeding.

In addition to regular observation methods several methods have been developed specifically for watching migration. One way of discovering night migrants that cannot be usually seen is watching migration facing the moon. You set up a pair of binoculars or a telescope on a tripod and direct it towards the moon, when it is at least three-quarters full. With a lot of patience the silhouettes of nocturnal migrants passing over the background of the moon can be discerned. One advantage of this method is that it can be used from inside the house, through an open window, and there is no need to go far to follow the birds...

Another good method for night observations is listening to birdcalls. Many species call out during migration, presumably for communication within the flock. Cranes, thrushes, geese, waders and songbirds use vocal communication frequently during migration. This is especially conspicuous in autumn, when most birds migrate for short periods of time and there are young birds in the flocks migrating for the first time. Juveniles call out more than adults, probably due to their lack of experience in flock migration.

In short, patience, experience and sometimes luck are needed to watch migrating birds. A sudden change in weather, for example, can cause significant alterations in migration routes and timing. Nevertheless, Israel is such a good site for watching migrating birds that with a bit of good will and perseverance it is possible to enjoy this wonderful natural phenomenon fully and enjoy every minute of it.

Birdwatchers watching migration in Eilat.
(Photo: Shraga Straj)

B. Where to Watch Birds

Watching migrating birds close to home is enjoyable, but a visit to one of the observation stations located along the major bird migration routes is a must. The chances of seeing large masses of migrants and a variety of species, both common and rare, are far greater in these areas.

Migrating birds fly along specific routes that facilitate their flight, such as the Syrian-African Rift or the Judean and Galilee Mountains, over which most soaring birds pass, or the Mediterranean coast, a major waterfowl and sea bird route. Specific sites along the route, used by migrants for feeding and resting are particularly useful for locating migrating birds and watching them. Shore and marsh birds use water bodies, other birds stop to rest and feed in fields and rural areas, woodlands and

Pages 200-201:
The Peregrine landing in its nest to feed its chicks is a raptor most of whose population migrates from the northern hemisphere to winter further south. Peregrines ringed in Russia have been found in Israel.
(Photo: P. De Med, Panda Photo)

Willem Van den Bossche, one of the volunteer birdwatchers who has come to Israel in the wake of migrating birds for five continuous seasons, watching autumn migration, as part of the joint study by the Israel Air Force and the SPNI. On his left is an army radio set to the only frequency in the Israel Defense Forces radio network on which eight different languages were spoken at one time. Willem worked in Israel for four years on his doctorate satellite tracking migrating storks in the Bet She'an Valley.
(Photo: Yossi Leshem)

forests that provide cover or roosting sites for many birds and in the desert, birds come to drink at seasonal pools and springs. Open areas (such as fields) and water bodies are especially suited for birdwatching, since unlike wooded areas, it is easy to find and watch the birds in the open. These are some of the best sites in Israel to see migrating birds:

Eilat is undoubtedly one the best places in Israel to watch migration and the greatest number of migrants and the largest variety of species in Israel can be found there, especially in spring, when it attracts masses of birds migrating from Africa to their breeding quarters in Europe and Asia. The variety of habitats in the Eilat vicinity that include beaches, ponds, fields and fruit tree groves, attract many migrants that stop to spend the night or even several days in the area. The International Birdwatching Center, located in the city, offers many activities for the public at large, including organized tours, guided birdwatching and numerous other pastimes. A self-guiding birdwatching path runs from the northern end of the Gulf of Eilat to the fields of Kibbutz Eilot via the salt pans. One of the major migration routes - the raptor "highway" - lies above the Eilat Mountains, from the Mt. Shlomo area, through Mt. Yo'ash, where tens of thousands of raptors can often be seen in one spring morning. There is a soaring bird route along the southern and central Arava Valley, and water birds and passerines can be seen along the entire length of the valley. Many of these birds stop to rest and feed in the area. The Arava, north of Eilat has several good birdwatching sites: Yotvata, En Yahav, Hatzeva and Idan. Kibbutz Lotan offers guided birdwatching tours, birding trails and lodging. Another important migration route passes over the Negev Mountains, and there is a good chance of seeing migrating birds, particularly in spring, in the Ramon Crater area and west of there towards Borot Lotz and the Egyptian border.

Many migrating birds can also be seen further north in the Negev. The area between Sede Boqer and Revivim and west of there, in the fields between Tse'elim and Urim, is a good spot to watch migrating soaring birds in spring and lies on one of the major White Stork migration routes. Further west in the northwestern Negev, between Tse'elim and Urim, many migrants come to winter in the area, including birds of prey, cranes and other birds. There is a major raptor and stork migration route over the Beersheba area and in the open spaces near the Negev Monument, on the Beersheba-Omer road, a variety of migrating passerines can be seen. The sewage plant south of the city attracts many water birds, both passage migrants and wintering birds. The Yeruham Reservoir, located west of the town of Yeruham, also attracts migrating water birds, as well as wintering and breeding species.

Another major soaring bird migration route lies over the Dead Sea Valley, and further north along the Jordan Valley. Raptors, storks and cranes fly over the En Gedi and Metsoke Dragot area on their way along the Fault Escarpment west of the Dead Sea. Many songbirds stop to rest and feed at the En Gedi oasis during migration. There are excellent soaring bird migration lookouts in the Metsoke Dragot area, above Nahal Dragot, or at Mitspeh Mikhvar, overlooking Nahal Hatsatson, where migrating birds can be seen flying by, above, below and alongside observers on the cliff. Another hot spot for raptor and stork migration is the Mt. of Temptation (Karantal) overlooking Jericho. Millions of different passerines also pass over the Dead Sea Valley, and can be seen, with water birds, at the various springs in the area.

West of the Syrian-African Rift, along the Judean and Samarian Mountains, lies another major soaring bird migration route used by most of the raptors, storks and White Pelicans migrating over Israel. There is an observation station and radar for watching and tracking migrating birds at the International Center for the Study of Bird Migration at Latrun. One of the first observation points, active for many years in the past, was in the Kfar Qasem area, along the western slopes of the Samarian Mountains. In the fields west of Kfar Qasem, a bit east of the road to Rosh Ha'ayin (Kesem Junction) birds of prey can be seen, mainly in autumn. Migration peaks include Honey Buzzard passage in the beginning of September, the Levant Sparrowhawk wave in the third week of September and Lesser Spotted Eagle migration between the end of September and the first week in October. Migrant raptors sometimes roost in wooded areas nearby such as the Koah forests.

The Mediterranean coast is a leading migration route for many sea and water birds. The Ma'agan Mikhael and Carmel coast area has many fish ponds that attract water

White Pelicans flying in formation.
(Photo: Noah Satat)

Migrating White Storks resting on the Mediterranean coast.
(Photo: Yig'al Livneh)

Observers in the SPNI's Northern Valleys migration survey: James P. Smith, whose line drawings appear in this book, is standing near the telescope. A Danish birdwatcher is talking on the radio, and behind him is Dan Alon, who has been coordinating the surveys for the past 12 years.
(Photo: Yossi Leshem)

Page 207:
Black Kites wintering in the Hula Valley
on the background of Mt. Hermon.
(Photo: Yossi Eshbol)

birds who come to rest and "refuel". The best time to visit the Ma'agan Mikhael Bird Sanctuary is autumn and winter, when water birds passing through and wintering in the area abound. The reserve is closed in spring to prevent disturbance to nesting birds. The Northern Valleys are also one of the major migration routes over Israel and a major soaring bird migration route lies over the Jezreel Valley. The soaring bird autumn migration survey has been held there by the SPNI since 1988, from the Alonim Junction in the west to Kfar Ruppin in the east. The main observation station is at Kibbutz Kfar Ruppin in the Bet-She'an Valley.

Many migrating and wintering birds of prey, storks and water birds can be seen in the Bet-She'an Valley. Some of the waterfowl also winter and even breed in the area. The SPNI and Kibbutz Kfar Ruppin have established the Jordan Valley International Birdwatching Center where the latest information on bird news in the area can be obtained. The center also runs a ringing station open to visitors and offers accommodations within easy walking distance of birdwatching sites.

There is also heavy soaring bird migration over the Upper Galilee Mountains, mainly in autumn, but in spring too. Honey Buzzards, Lesser Spotted Eagles and other species fly over the Naftali Mountains, Mt. Meron and Mt. Canaan.

The Hula Valley is undoubtedly one of the most important sites for watching birds in Israel. The Hula Nature Reserve, as well as the many fields and ponds in the valley north of the reserve, attract a variety of water birds, raptors and many other species. The valley attracts migrants in autumn and spring, and is one of the major wintering concentrations of raptors and water birds in Israel.

The area north of the reserve was flooded in the last decade and water birds abound. During the winter dozens of Spotted and Imperial Eagles, about 20,000 Cranes and many other species can be seen in the surrounding fields. The site can be reached by a road that turns east about three kilometers north of the Hula Reserve. Bet Ussishkin, a small nature museum at Kibbutz Dan east of Qiryat Shemona has specimens of many of the characteristic birds of the area, an audio-visual presentation on the Hula Valley and provides the latest news on where and what birds to see in the Hula Valley. In the Golan Heights the Gamla Nature Reserve is probably one of the best sites to watch migration both in autumn and in spring. Dozens of Griffon Vultures, Bonelli's Eagle, Egyptian Vultures, Short-toed Eagles and Eagle Owls nest in the lush, majestic landscape. This is definitely a site worth a half-day of birding that combines watching resident species with migration overhead.

The Israel Knesset is probably the only parliament in the world with its own bird ringing (banding) station. In the gardens surrounding the Knesset, near the helicopter landing pad, a bird observatory that includes a permanent ringing station has been established. These gardens, a large green spot in the heart of Jerusalem attract many migrating songbirds. Anyone visiting Jerusalem should try to spend a few hours at the station (visits should be arranged in advance).

A Steppe Buzzard photographed while stopping to rest at En Gedi.
(Photo: Ofer Bahat)

C. Migration Dates

Bird migration of some magnitude can be seen almost any time of the year at various sites in Israel. However, in order to see the massive migration waves, the best time is the peak of spring or autumn migration. Every species usually migrates at relatively constant dates every year. In spring most migration is concentrated in March and April, although early migrants, such as adult Steppe Eagles pass over Israel in mid-February, while Honey Buzzards, the last migrants in spring, pass over mainly in the first half of May.

In autumn, migration is usually spread over a longer time period, although there is still a clear peak in September and October. The first autumn migrants, such as Honey Buzzards and storks pass over Israel in the end of August. The last migrants, such as pelicans or Steppe Eagles migrate in November.

The table below presents data on passage times of soaring birds migrating over Israel that can be useful for planning migration watching. The data were summarized from nine years of research in the joint study with the Israel Air Force.

206

Passage time periods for several species during autumn migration

Species	Passage of first 5% of the population	Passage of 90% of the population	Passage of last 5% of the population	Average passage day
Honey Buzzard	17.8 - 29.8	14.9 - 30.8	15.9 - 15.10	7.9
Levant Sparrowhawk	1.9 - 13.9	14.9 - 26.9	27.9 - 17.10	21.9
Lesser Spotted Eagle	22.8 - 20.9	21.9 - 5.10	6.10 - 17.10	1.10
White Stork	1.8 - 15.8	16.8 - 12.9	13.9 - 31.10	21.8
Pelican	17.7 - 17.9	18.9 - 7.11	8.11 - 20.11	26.10
Black Kite	22.8 - 30.8	31.8 - 4.10	5.10 - 13.10	9.9
Steppe Eagle	26.9 - 12.10	13.10 - 1.11	2.11 - 29.11	23.10

Passage time periods for several species during spring migration

Species	Passage of first 5% of the population	Passage of 90% of the population	Passage of last 5% of the population	Average passage day
Steppe Eagle	14.2 - 22.2	23.2 - 27.3	28.3 - 17.5	10.3
Steppe Buzzard	25.2 - 21.3	22.3 - 15.4	16.4 - 24.5	31.3
Black Kite	2.3 - 20.3	21.3 - 10.4	11.4 - 31.5	29.3
Levant Sparrowhawk	9.3 - 17.4	18.4 - 26.4	27.4 - 18.5	24.4
Honey Buzzard	20.4 - 1.5	2.5 - 12.5	13.5 - 25.5	9.5
White Stork	1.3 - 13.3	14.3 - 25.4	21.5 - 26.4	28.3

Remembering main passage dates and the migration route of each species makes chances for seeing it quite good. Nevertheless, during the principal migration months, at major migration sites, there are usually at least some migrating birds, so a birdwatching trip to follow migration in Israel is relatively easy to plan.

Steppe Eagles and a Lesser Spotted Eagle on migration.
(Drawing: James P. Smith)

An F-15 fighter plane flying over the snow-covered Ramon Crater in the Negev Desert.
(Photo: courtesy of the Israel Air Force)

Pages 210-211:
White Pelicans flying in formation.
(Drawing: James P. Smith)

כַּנֶּשֶׁר יִדְאֶה וּפָרַשׂ כְּנָפָיו (ירמיהו מ״ח, מ)

"Behold, he shall fly like a vulture,
and shall spread his wings..."
(Jeremiah, 48:40)

A. *The Bird Migration Center at Latrun, Israel - Beating Swords Into Ploughshares*

In the heart of Israel, at the foot of the Jerusalem Hills overlooking the Ayalon Valley and the Coastal Plain, midway between Tel-Aviv and Jerusalem, next to the main highway (Route 1) and 18 km southeast of the Ben-Gurion International Airport, lies Latrun. In 1995 the Society for the Protection of Nature in Israel (SPNI) and Tel-Aviv University initiated the establishment of the International Center for the Study of Bird Migration at the Armored Corps Memorial in Latrun.

The Latrun area is renowned since the days of the Bible: in the adjacent Ayalon Valley, Joshua fought the famous battle during which "the sun stood still, and the moon stayed" (Joshua, 10:12) and many years later Judah Maccabee fought the Battle of Emaus nearby. It was also one of the most important crossroads in the Middle East, where the roads from Jaffa to Jerusalem and from Gaza to Ramallah and Damascus, met. Close to the site is one of the largest Crusader castles in the Middle East. During the War of Independence, the first armored battle in Israeli history was fought over the control of the strategically located British police fort at Latrun that dominated the road to besieged Jerusalem. The Israel Armored Corps has established a memorial at Latrun to honor the memory of the 4,855 Armored Corps soldiers who gave their lives in Israel's wars. The memorial includes a museum with an open-air exhibition of 150 tanks, one of the largest of its kind in the world. The site, with it unique history and convenient location attracts many visitors and in 1998 alone, close to a half-million people - families, soldiers, schoolchildren and tourists - visited the site.

A flock of White Pelicans flying off on migration.
(Photo: Yig'al Livneh)

Israel's unique location at the junction of three continents makes it an international crossroads for migrating birds: some 500 million birds cross Israel's skies heading south to Africa in autumn and then flying north to Europe and Asia in the spring. Over the years several major migration routes have been mapped over Israel. Latrun is located at the very heart of the western migration route, which lies along the foothills of the Judean and Samarian Mountains.

The board of the Armored Corps Memorial at Latrun have allocated Tel-Aviv University and the Society for the Protection of Nature in Israel (SPNI) an area of eight acres on the western side of the site for the establishment of the International Center for the Study of Bird Migration. Tel-Aviv University currently leads the research institute at the complex and will hopefully be joined in the future by other academic institutions so the center will become an inter-university project. An MRL-5 weather radar, purchased in Russia was brought to Latrun in 1996 and is operated by Dr. Leonid Dinewitz who immigrated to Israel from Moldavia.

A 250-seat auditorium and an interactive museum will be built at the site. Visitors will be able to hear, see and actively participate in exhibits illustrating the theme of migration, the joint research project with the IAF and how peaceful coexistence between migrating birds and aircraft was achieved.

The center would not have become a reality without the generous help of four sponsors: the Samis Foundation from Seattle funded the Samuel Israel Auditorium; Moshe Yanai, an Israeli from Kfar Yehezqel, vice-president of EMC [2] in Boston will fund the interactive museum to be named for his parents Rachel and David Yundler;

Page 212:
White Storks land to roost during migration.
(Photo: Yig'al Livneh)

213

The Armored Corps Memorial in Latrun: in the center is the British Police Station, around which Israel's first armored battle was fought during the War of Independence. To the right of the police station is a memorial wall for 4,855 fallen Armored Corps soldiers. Around the square is an exhibition of 150 tanks. On the upper left is the research radar (red and white) and below it the amphitheater that can seat 13,000.
(Upper photo: Yossi et Uzi Ltd.)

Sunset over the MRL-5 radar of the International Center for the Study of Bird Migration at the Armored Corps Memorial in Latrun.
(Lower photo: Yossi Leshem)

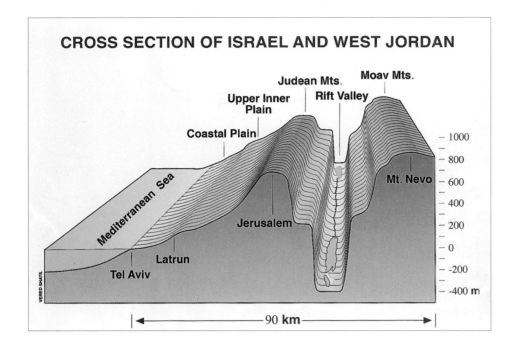

CROSS SECTION OF ISRAEL AND WEST JORDAN

Judean Mts. Moav Mts.

Upper Inner   Rift Valley
Plain

Coastal Plain

Mediterranean Sea

Mt. Nevo

Jerusalem

Latrun

Tel Aviv

- 1000
- 800
- 600
- 400
- 200
- 0
- -200
- -400 m

|←————— 90 km —————→|

Lockheed Martin is helping advance the construction of classrooms and educational themes and the Israel Tourist Corporation is helping with planning and infrastructure.

A joint educational center for the Armored Corps Association and the SPNI is now being built and will have 50 rooms, classrooms and a dining hall for students, soldiers and nature lovers from Israel and abroad.

The conceptual purpose of the project is to combine history - the Armored Corps Museum and the battles fought around Latrun in the past - with the future: bird migration, flight safety, environmental protection and education. A campground is planned adjacent to the field study center and will serve as a focal point for youth and adult nature activities such as birdwatching, hikes, orienteering and conservation of the surrounding environment. Landscaping at the field study center will focus on vegetation that attracts birds and nest boxes and feeding perches will be placed throughout the area, following the tradition developed in Europe and North America. A park of native Israeli trees and species mentioned in the Bible will be planted in memory of the late Prime Minister Yitzhak Rabin, on an adjacent 55 acre site, and will be part of the Armored Corps Park. All these will contribute to making the entire area a center for education and conservation unlike any other in the Middle East.

Numerous statesmen, the media and over 3000 members of the public attended the groundbreaking ceremony that took place on October 1, 1995. The complex will

Educational activity at the Latrun amphitheater: 13,000 young people gather at the site after a day of hiking in the area. The bird radar can be seen in the background.
(Photo: Yossi et Uzi Ltd.)

Pages 216-217:
Migrating Spanish Sparrows near Eilat.
(Photo: Yossi Eshbol)

215

November 1995: Two days before Prime Minister Yitzhak Rabin was assassinated he visited the Armored Corps Memorial at Latrun. Mr. Rabin can be seen here at the "Wall of Names" where the names of 4855 fallen from the Armored Corps are inscribed. At his right is Major General (res.) Musa Peled, chairman of the Armored Corps Association. As he was standing at the memorial wall Rabin said that he estimated that he had more friends on the wall than in life.
(Photo: Yossi et Uzi Ltd.)

be named after the late Sergeant Nachshon Wachsmann, who was kidnapped and murdered by terrorists in October 1994, and the late Captain Nir Poraz, who was killed in the attempt to rescue Wachsmann. The decision to dedicate a center devoted to education, conservation and flight safety in the land Nir and Nachshon loved, to their memory, symbolizes the fact that terror must stop, that the time has come to look ahead to a new era of peace, as in the motto of our project: "Migrating Birds Know No Boundaries".

The large amounts of information and data gathered on bird migration over the past two decades, combined with the unique position of the Middle East and Israel at the junction of three continents, provide a singular opportunity to establish an international center for the study of bird migration. The center has great potential for interdisciplinary activity in a number of fields that can help promote additional ties between the countries of the Middle East, as well as ties with Europe, west Asia and Africa, and with the Jewish communities all over the world.

On October 17, 1973, during the Yom Kippur War, on the Jewish festival of Simhat Torah, Major Ma'oz Poraz's Skyhawk fighter plane was downed by a missile over the Suez Canal on the shores of the Great Bitter Lake. Ma'oz was 39 when he was killed. About five years earlier, on July 23 1968, he was copilot to Oded Abarbanel when an El-Al flight from Italy to Israel was highjacked by three Arab terrorists. Poraz tried to resist, and was wounded when one of the terrorists hit him in the stomach with his rifle butt. This was the first highjacking during the Middle Eastern conflict, and the plane landed in Algeria. The hostages were released only at the end of August, following massive international pressure, in exchange for dozens of terrorists Israel released. Ma'oz was angered by the deal, and when he returned, claimed that Israel should never have given in to the terrorist demands.

Twenty-six years later, on the principle of not giving in to terrorist demands, Captain Nir Poraz, the son of Ma'oz and Mati, led a commando force to attempt to rescue Sergeant Nachshon Wachsmann who had been kidnapped several days earlier by terrorists.

218

Sergeant Nachshon Wachsmann from Jerusalem served in the Golani brigade. He was kidnapped and killed by terrorists on October 14, 1994 at the age of 19. He loved nature, hikes and his country.

Captain Nir Poraz from Ramat Hasharon served in the elite Matkal Commando Unit. He fell in the line of duty during the mission to rescue Nachshon Wachsmann from terrorists on October 14, 1994, at the age of 22. He loved orienteering, traveling, nature and his country.

October 1, 1995, inauguration ceremony of the Migration Center at Latrun: Mrs. Mati Poraz, whose husband, Major Ma'oz, an IAF fighter pilot, fell in the Yom Kippur War and whose son Nir fell in the battle to free Sergeant Nachshon Wachsmann, standing next to Nachshon's father, Yehuda Wachsmann (Tzvi Bar, Mayor of Ramat-Gan is behind them).

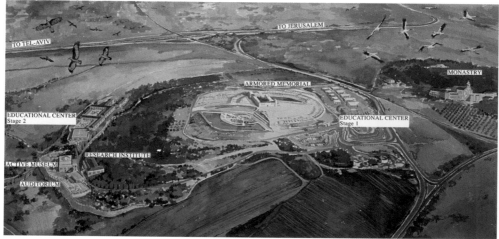

The Latrun memorial overlooks the Ayalon Valley where many battles were fought from the days of Joshua when sun stood still. This sunset was photographed from the bird radar on 24 November 1997 and brings to mind the verse from the Book of Joshua (10:12): "Sun, stand still upon Gibeon; and you, Moon, in the valley of Ayalon".
(Upper photo: Yossi Leshem)

First stages in the plans for the International Center for the Study of Bird Migration at Latrun and its position in relation to the Armored Corps Memorial.
(Lower drawing: Architect - Nili Portugali)

B. Satellites Research

Israel's unique location as a bottleneck along the migration route provides excellent conditions for all aspects of bird migration research due to the huge numbers of birds flying over the country. The International Center for the Study of Bird Migration aims to bring together researchers from Europe and western Asia, where the birds breed, from the Middle East over which they migrate, and from Africa, where they winter.

A New Era - Using Satellites to Map Migration Routes

Joint German-Israeli research on bird migration has been going on since 1994 funded by the German Ministry for the Environment, Nature Conservation and Nuclear Safety. The project is a cooperative venture between the Max Planck Institute in Vogelwarte Radolfzell in Germany and Tel-Aviv University and the SPNI in Israel. Research focuses on migrating White Storks and uses satellite transmitters to follow the birds and track their migration routes.

Radio-telemetry is widely used in biological research and is intended principally for locating animals in their natural environment. This method enables physiological and behavioral data on animals to be gathered and serves as an important instrument for managing nature reserves and in studies aimed at saving rare animals or returning them to nature. Biologists usually use minute transmitters in the VHF range, usually with frequencies between 150 and 152 megahertz, that allow them to use small, portable receivers that are easy to carry in the field. For animals moving rapidly across large spaces (such as migrating birds) however, the limited receiving range in this frequency range is a serious shortcoming.

In 1984 modern technology first made it practical to use satellites for tracking birds, with the development of transmitters small enough to be carried by a medium-sized bird without interfering with its normal behavior and ability to fly.

The Argos satellite data collection and location system is run jointly by the French space research agency (CNES), the American agency for oceanic and atmospheric research (NOAA) and space agency (NASA). The system includes transmitters, equipment on Tiros satellites that receives signals from the various transmitters during the 28 orbits they make a day, and ground stations for communicating with the satellites, analyzing the transmitted data and transferring it to the various elements using the transmitters. The Argos system was originally developed for locating objects such as buoys at sea, floating meteorological stations and oil drill barges. Only in its later stages was the system used for tracking animal movements, including their migration across the globe.

The system locates the transmitter using the Doppler principle: as a result of the movement of the satellite relative to the transmitter, the transmitting frequency changes. As the satellite approaches the transmitter, the frequency received by the satellite is a bit higher than the frequency originally transmitted. The frequency received is lower than it was originally transmitted when the satellite passes the transmitter and moves away from it. When the frequency transmitted by the transmitter and the frequency received by the satellite are identical, the satellite is exactly perpendicular to the transmitter. In order to locate the transmitter, the satellite must receive at least four consecutive transmissions during each orbit. The location accuracy is at least 3000 meters, and usually between 300 and 1000 meters. Thus, this system enables excellent tracking of migrating birds all over the globe. During the last decade, satellite transmitters working with the Argos system have been used to follow many bird species such as swans, eagles, cranes, pelicans, petrels, albatrosses and storks. The transmitters have become so miniaturized that they weigh as little as 16.5 grams, which allows them to be used for studying relatively small birds. (A bird can comfortably carry a transmitter weighing up to four percent of its weight.)

The first experiment in tracking a bird using the Argos system took place in 1984. A transmitter was attached to a Bald Eagle in the northern Chesapeake Bay on the East Coast of the United States on 20 July 1984. The eagle migrated south along the coast until it reached its wintering grounds in Florida where transmissions were picked up on 6 December 1984. The satellite made it possible to receive accurate

White Stork which has been caught and equiped with satellite received tag while wintering in the Beit-Shean Valley in late 1993. During April 1994, the bird returned to its breeding area near Kiev, Ukraine, after traveling a distance of 2,600 kilometers.
(Photo: Dan Alon)

The transmitter attached to the stork's back emits signals into space that are received by the ARGOS satellite and transmitted to the computation center at Tolouse in France. From there data are transmitted via the Internet to our scientific center and later to the educational program developed by the SPNI, Ministry of Education and Tel-Aviv University, so schoolchildren can constantly follow migration routes of storks, cranes, vultures, eagles and pelicans.
(Upper drawing: Adth van Ooijen)

Page 222:
Willem Van den Bossche, the Belgian Ph.D. student and Kobi Merom, from Kibbutz Nir David, one of the foremost Israeli bird ringers attaching a radio-transmitter to a migrating White Stork in the Beit-Shean Valley, Israel.
(Opposite photo: Benaya Bin-Nun)

A pair of first year migrating White Storks with satellite received transmitters attached on their way south to Africa in the autumn.
(Photo: Thomas Bich)

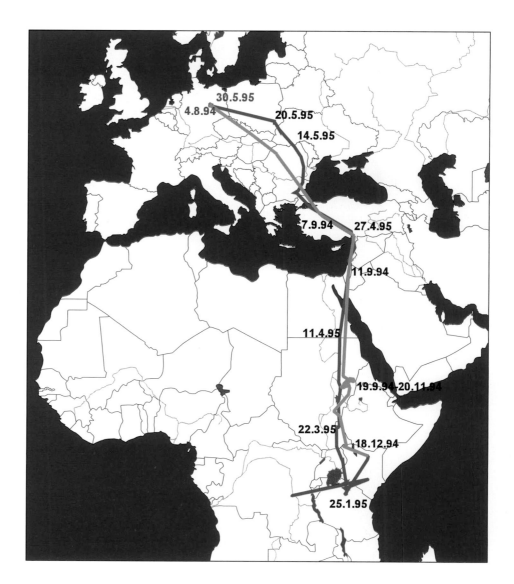

This is an example of the entire migration route of a white stork named Princessen tracked by children through the Internet program "Migrating birds Know No Boundaries" from April 1994 through May 1995. The green route is the southbound migration from Europe and Africa during 1994 and the red route is for 1995, when the stork returned to the same nest.

These are five White Stork migration routes from their nesting sites in Germany to their wintering sites in Africa, representing 77 White Storks that were fitted with satellite transmitters as part of a joint German-Israeli research program. Several of these birds can be followed in real-time through the Internet.

The second phase of the project is being led by Judy Shamoun-Baranes who is developing a Geographic Information System (GIS) based model of bird migration, integrating all the available data on soaring bird migration in the region into one database.

The stork Siegfried (green route), migrated away from the regular route along the eastern part of the Red Sea and was shot by a Yemenite officer. The transmitter was later returned to Germany.

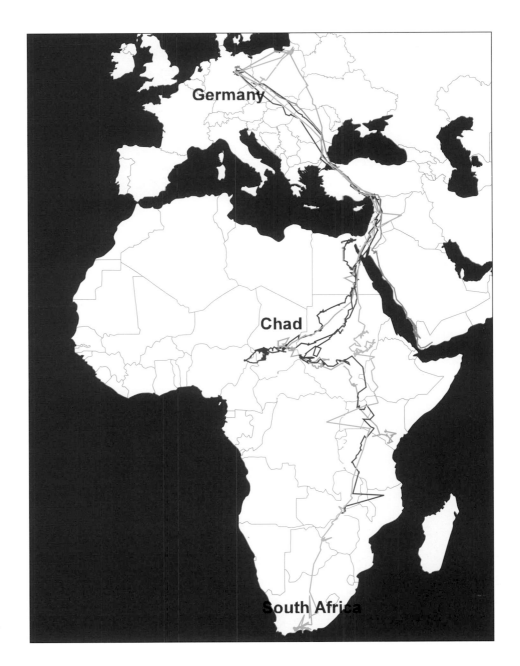

The moon rises on a migrating stork, with a satellite-received transmitter attached, stopping to rest for the night. (Photo: Michael Kaatz)

225

Prof. Bernd Meyburg from Germany holding a Steppe Eagle he caught in Saudi-Arabia and to which he fitted a back-pack satellite received transmitter.

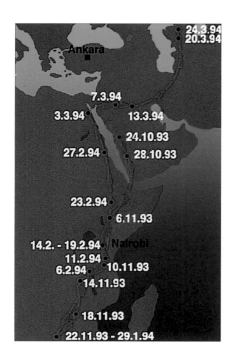

The route of a Steppe Eagle which has been radio tagged by Prof. Bernd Meyburg and was followed by the Argos satellites from Saudi-Arabia to Africa in the autumn and back in the spring through Eilat, to its nest in Kazachstan. (Courtesy: B. Meyburg)

The map is part of the development of a GIS-based bird migration model for the Middle-East, shows the migration routes of White Storks fitted with satellite received transmitters over Turkey. These data will be used by the Turkish, Israel, US, NATO Air Forces, to avoid collisions with migrating birds.

226

data on the route of a migrating bird for the first time ever, without ground-based tracking. The transmitter was attached to the eagle's back with a harness and the antenna pointed back, towards the bird's tail. This method is used for attaching transmitters to birds to this day.

Six male Wandering Albatrosses had satellite transmitters attached to them on the island of Crozet, halfway between South Africa to Antarctica. Four of the six were followed for about a month, while wandering around the oceans looking for food. One albatross covered a distance of 10,427 kilometers during 27 days. The satellite located it 314 times and its maximal flight velocity between location points was 63 kilometers per hour. Another albatross flew a total of 15,200 kilometers during 33 days. The satellite located it successfully 385 times and its maximal flight velocity between location points was 81 kilometers per hour. On one of the days it was tracked this albatross covered a total of 936 kilometers!

Four Whooper Swans, one female and three males, had transmitters attached on 10 April 1990, on Hokkaido Island in northern Japan. The swans were on their way from their wintering grounds in Japan, north to their breeding grounds in Russia. They migrated north, past the Sakhalin Isles, towards the delta of the Amur River in eastern Russia, where they stopped to rest and then continued on their way. One of the swans, a female, was followed until it reached the Whooping Swan breeding grounds in northeastern Siberia near the North Sea, in mid-May 1990. It had covered a distance of 3083 kilometers during its migration and was seen back in Japan in mid-November of that year, accompanied by a young swan - one of its young - that had migrated with it mother from the nest it hatched in, to their wintering grounds in Japan.

In spring of 1989, transmitters weighing 45 grams were attached to three White Storks with special harnesses. Professor Udo Renner and Amnon Ginati from Berlin University, along with Yossi Leshem and Israel Ornithology Center staff, trapped three migrating storks in the area of Kibbutz Tse'elim in the western Negev. The storks were released after having transmitters attached and were tracked using the motorized glider. This preliminary experiment showed beyond a doubt that the transmitter does not hinder the storks that can soar and glide normally with other storks in a thermal. A special antenna was attached to the underside of the glider to receive the transmitter signals and locate the storks.

Following this successful trial, the SPNI, Tel-Aviv University and the Max Planck Institute at Radolfzell in Germany proposed a research project that received funding from the German Ministry for the Environment, Nature Conservation and Nuclear Safety. Professor Peter Berthold and Dr. Eugenius Nowak from Germany and Dr. Yossi Leshem from Israel led the project. The aim of the study was to follow White Storks migrating from Germany to Africa via Israel, by attaching satellite-received transmitters. Willem Van den Bossche, a Belgian student, did his Ph.D. thesis on storks

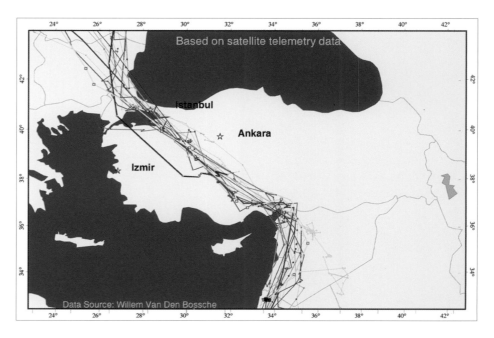

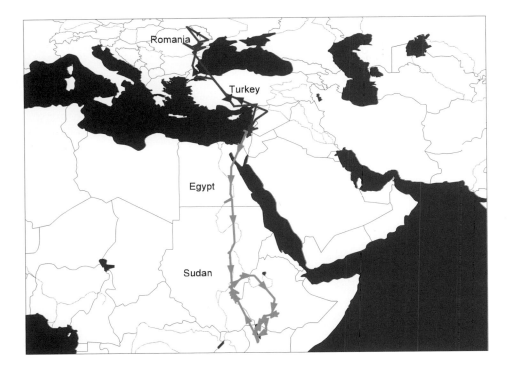

Satellite telemetry data from Marva Shmueli's White Pelican migration research project. The pelican "Freddie" (green route - October 96 - December 97) is a young pelican that was found exhausted in Tel-Aviv on November 11 1996 and released shortly afterward. The second pelican is named "Martin" (red route - January 95 - March 96).

This pelican that had a transmitter attached in the Jezreel Valley fields flies off. This is the first pelican in the world with a transmitter attached that was tracked in migration down to the Sud marshes in Sudan as part of Marva Shmueli's study.
(Photo: Marva Shmueli)

wintering and migrating in Israel, particularly in the Bet She'an Valley area. At the same time, Michael Kaatz, a German student, began tracking the storks with transmitters attached, in Germany, using light aircraft to fly with them southeast to the Bosphorus Straits in Turkey.

Between 1994 and 1999 transmitters were attached to 77 White Storks, juveniles and adults, in Germany and in Israel. The experiment provided valuable information on a variety of subjects: the exact routes the storks migrate along, their daily rate of progress (in ideal conditions the exact location of the bird is transmitted every 90 minutes), how wintering and migratory strategies are related to the availability of food, and how weather affects the route and rate of migration.

The preferred stopover sites were studied as a basis for formulating conservation policy on which sites to protect. The first stage of data analysis was completed in 1997 based on the information gathered in both Ph.D. theses. The German Ministry for the Environment approved a research budget for an additional three years (1997-1999) so a clearer picture of the migration process could to be obtained.

Analysis of the data relating to another stork (number 94543) provides information on the daily progress rate from Germany to Sudan. This stork sometimes flew up to 515 kilometers on a single day. It started off in Germany, stopped for ten days in the Bet-She'an Valley in Israel, between 15 and 25 September, and then continued on to Sudan.

Tracking animals with the help of radio telemetry has advanced considerably over the past decade. Transmitters have been miniaturized from 150 grams to 17 grams. At this pace, if the current rate of technological progress continues, we should be seeing micro-transmitters weighing only one or two grams by the first decade of the next century. This will enable tracking of even smaller animals and will increase the number of bird species whose migration can be followed using telemetry. Transmitters powered by solar batteries have been developed during the past few years, so the same bird can be tracked for several years. Microwave Telemetry Inc. from Maryland in the United States, managed by Dr. Paul Howey, is one of the leading developers in the field. As these pages are being written (1999) a transmitter with GPS weighing 170 grams is almost on the market.

In addition to the large stork-tracking project, Dr. Bernd Meyburg is using telemetry to follow different eagle species, including Spotted Eagles, Lesser Spotted Eagles, Short-toed Eagles, Ospreys, Imperial Eagles and Steppe Eagles. Many of these migrate over Israel and the Middle East. Few years ago Dr. Ido Izhaki and Marva Shmueli have started research involving telemetry on White Pelicans and have succeeded for the first time ever to follow a migrating White Pelican to its wintering areas in Sudan.

One of the newspaper articles that reported the pelican with a transmitter caught by the Sudanians as the bird "spying for the Israeli Mossad".

227

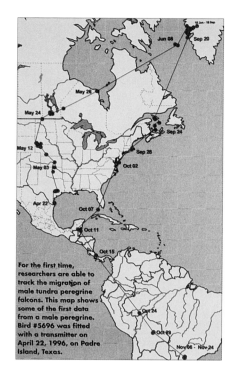

For the first time, researchers are able to track the migration of male tundra peregrine falcons. This map shows some of the first data from a male peregrine. Bird #5696 was fitted with a transmitter on April 22, 1996, on Padre Island, Texas.

The migration route of a Peregrine from Greenland via the eastern coast of the United States down to South America (Courtesy of Dr. William S. Seegar). About 30 other researchers follow migration with satellite telemetry all over the world.

About 20,000 Cranes winter each year in the Hula Valley since 1990. Dan Alon studies the wintering crane populations and attaches satellite transmitters to them.
This Crane is equiped with a back-pack transmitter and colored rings on its legs for individual identification in the field. The project is financed by Lufthansa, the German airline whose symbol is a crane in flight.
(Photo: Ephi Sharir)

In December 1998 Dan Alon attached satellite-transmitters to four Cranes in the Hula Valley as part of his study on wintering Cranes in the Hula Valley. The study is being done with two of the leading researchers in this field, Professor Javier Alonso and Professor Juan Carlos Alonso. The number of wintering Cranes in the Hula Valley has reached 20,000 in the past decade, which has made the Hula one of the foremost wintering sites for Cranes.

In 1995, Ofer Bahat and Ohad Hatzofe decided to use satellite telemetry for tracking resident birds of prey in Israel. They attached transmitters to six Griffon Vultures, to compare data between migrating and resident birds. One of the birds was named "Freedom" by Batya Arad, the mother of Ron Arad, a Phantom F-4 navigator in captivity since 1986. Surprisingly, "Freedom" was found to wander around the Middle East. A total of 180 satellite locations were received during two months between May and June 1995. They showed that "Freedom" flew 227 kilometers into Syria, entered Jordan eight times and Lebanon once, wandered around the Carmel in Israel, and spent most of its time in the Nahal Gamla area in the Golan Heights. Three immature Griffon Vultures tracked by satellite were found to have wandered from Israel to Turkey and returned to Israel after a while.

In North America too, satellite telemetry is being used for studying migration of raptors and other large birds between the Americas. Eventually it will be possible to compare the data between the Old and the New World along the two migration axes: Eurasia - Africa and North - Central - South America.

228

Three Griffon Vultures in formation flight over the Gamla Nature Reserve in the Golan Heights can be a model for any pilot.

(Photo: Ofer Bahat)

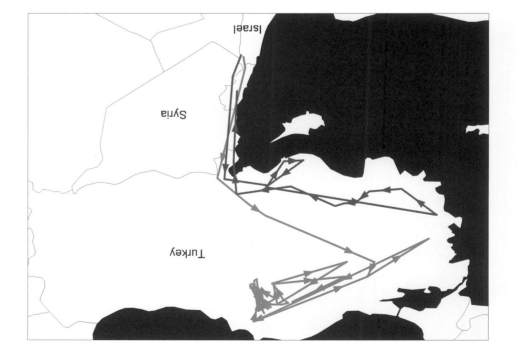

Satellite telemetry data, from Dr. Ofer Bahat's long term research program, for two Griffon Vultures, Saki (purple route) and Woodly (green route), that made long distance flights to Turkey and back to Israel.
(Saki April 13 to May 11 1995, Woodly April 29 to September 9, 1998).

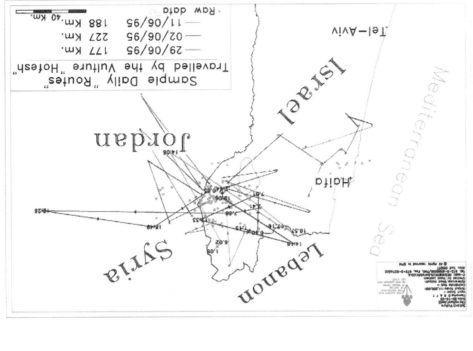

Sample Daily "Routes"
Travelled by the Vulture "Hotesh"

—— 29/06/95	177	Km.
—— 02/06/95	227	Km.
—— 11/06/95	188	Km.

40 Km.

Raw data.

The movements of "Freedom" - the wandering Griffon Vulture - in the Middle East during May-June 1995, showing flights from Israel into Syria, Jordan and Lebanon.
(Courtesy: Ohad Hatzofe).

A Griffon Vulture with a transmitter in flight. Note the bleached flight feathers and the colored rings on its legs that allow it to be individually identified in the field.
(Photo: Ofer Bahat)

Prof. Javier Alonso holding a Crane with a transmitter attached to its back
on the background of the Jordan River in the Hula Valley.
(Photo: Ephi Sharir)

C. Establishment of a Radar Network in the Middle East

The radar at Ben-Gurion International Airport, (which was described in chapter 4, section G), played a major role in the migration research program for the Israel Air Force. With the help of radar we were able to do an in-depth study of migration route fluctuations in real time, in the coastal plain area between Hadera in the north to Beersheba in the south. Nevertheless, air force radars are unable to follow bird movements in other parts of the country, so real time bird movements could not be followed in the Galilee and Golan in the north, or in the Negev and Judean Desert in the south, and maneuvering aircraft could not be warned.

On 10 August 1995 an F-15 fighter plane crashed after hitting three storks and the pilot and navigator were killed. The commander of the Israel Air Force decided to establish a bird and weather radar network across the country that could provide real time warning on birds' position and altitude in an attempt to substantially reduce the probability of collisions with migrating and wintering birds. Moreover, on days with no migration (40-50% of the migration season) it would be possible to fly and maneuver at low altitudes even at the height of the migration season. In addition it would be possible to study the appearance of the first migrating flocks before BPZ regulations go into effect, and to locate "late" flocks, that appear after the migration season is over.

In the 1980's and early 1990's, over 850,000 Jews emigrated from Russia to Israel. One of the new immigrants was a brigadier general, Dr. Leonid Dinewitz, who had been in command of a network of 45 MRL-5 weather radars in Russia that had been used for meteorological studies and artificial rain production.

The SPNI contacted Dr. Dinewitz and provided him with lodgings at the Har Gilo Field Study Center. The Hebrew University in Jerusalem offered him a position and later Tel-Aviv University as well. The Hebrew University financed the purchase of one of the radars from Russia, which due to the rampant inflation there was purchased at a "bargain price" and brought, with no little difficulty, to the Armored Corps Memorial at Latrun, with the help of the Ministry of Science and Technology. It is a two-frequency radar, three and ten centimeters, so both weather changes and bird movements can be studied.

The radar was placed at the Armored Corps Memorial at Latrun and inaugurated in the presence of the Israeli President, Mr. Ezer Weizman and the Minister of the Environment, Mr. Yossi Sarid in spring 1996 (see photo). The radar is used for studying migration and for presenting the subject to the public visiting the site. In the auditorium to be built visitors will be able to watch migrating flocks and receive a computer printout with real-time maps of flock locations in the Coastal Plain area. They can then travel with these printouts to watch migration within a radius of dozens of kilometers around the migration research center at Latrun.

The Israel Air Force is now (March 1999) in the final stages of examining and purchasing a new generation of Doppler radar (NEXRAD) for detecting birds. The American National Weather Service, along with the Federal Aviation Authority (FAA)

14 September 1996:
Mr. Ezer Weizman, President of Israel and Mr. Yossi Sarid, Minister of the Environment, at the inauguration ceremony for the new Russian MRL-5 radar at Latrun.
(Photo: Yossi et Uzi Ltd.)

The Russian MRL-5 radar at the Armored Corps Memorial, Latrun. In front of the radar are two Israeli manufactured Chariot (Merkava in Hebrew) Tanks.
(Photo: Yossi Leshem)

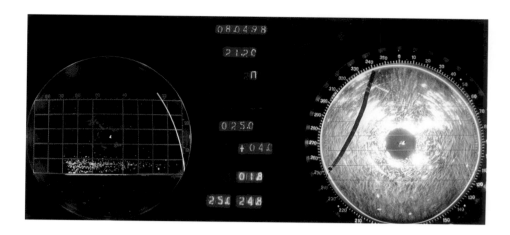

Massive night migration as seen on the MRL-5 radar at Latrun on 8 April 1998 at 2120 h. On the upper right the entire area is covered by migrating bird flocks; in the center of the screen is Latrun, and the red line is the Mediterranean coast. On the upper left is a vertical section of the flocks on the right hand photo. On the RHI screen each square is 2.5X2.5 km. The major mass of migration is concentrated up to an altitude of about 2.5 km. (Photo: Dr. L. Dinewitz)

Dr. Leonid Dinewitz immigrated to Israel from Moldavia in the former Soviet Union where he was a three-star general operating a network of 45 weather radars. Dr. Dinewitz came to Israel with the large Jewish immigration wave in 1991 and now leads the radar research at Latrun.

and the Department of Defense have invested 2.7 billion dollars and established a network of 165 NEXRAD radar all over the continent in order to predict and follow climatic changes. These radars are manufactured by Lockheed Martin and are able to identify bird migration.

If these radars are found to be appropriate, Israel will purchase them too, with the aim of setting up a network of weather and bird radars throughout the Middle East. A joint radar network spread over Turkey, Jordan and Egypt has the potential, with the progress of the peace process in the area, to distinctly increase both civilian and military flight safety. During autumn migration the Turkish Air Force radar can provide Jordan and Israel with warnings on approaching migration waves two days in advance and Israel in turn can warn Egypt of approaching migration. In spring the situation would be reversed: Egypt would warn Israel, who in turn would warn Jordan. Turkey could thus be warned two days in advance about the approach of migrating flocks.

The problem of damage to military aircraft from birds is serious in all air forces. The United States Air Force (USAF), for example, loses an average of 14 planes annually during its normal activity, three of which are results of birdstrike.

The USAF Colorado Springs Academy is in the final stages of developing a BAM (Bird Avoidance Model). The model is based on a geographical information system (GIS) framework that will include biological, climatic and environmental data, in order to predict what areas are potentially sensitive. As a result of the Israeli initiative a cooperative venture between the IAF and the USAF has been started. The Americans will develop the model for North America, and Judy Shamoun-Baranes, an Israeli scientist working towards her Ph.D. at Tel-Aviv University, will study how the model can be applied in the Middle East and Europe.

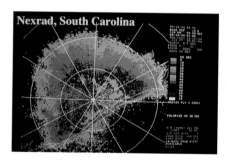

In the upper photo, heavy migration (blue) of birds across the Gulf of Mexico in the early evening is seen as tracked by a NEXRAD radar.
The photo on the right shows the national network of 165 NEXRAD radars in the USA. The compressed reflection of heavy migration follows a front on 4.10.95 at 04:26. (Photos: S.A. Gauthreaux Jr.)

A year after the Jordanian-Israeli peace treaty was signed, an IAF F-15 and a RJAF F-5 in a joint salutation flight over the Dead Sea and Jordan Valley the peace border.
(Upper photo: Courtesy of the Israel Air Force)

22 June 1998 - A delegation of senior Royal Jordanian Air Force pilots visiting the Armored Corps Memorial and the International Center for the Study of Bird Migration at Latrun. The guests and hosts from the IAF against the background of the Russian bird radar, with the Israeli and Jordanian flags flying together.
(Lower photo: Adiv Gal)

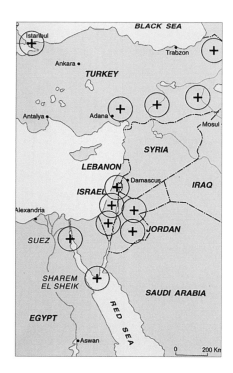

A radar network in the Middle East will allow the cooperation between air forces in the region to advance and develop a regional warning system for migrating bird movements.
(Courtesy: Vered Shatil)

Research done by Adiv Gal allows migrating bird calls to be tracked at night at the same time they are followed by the Latrun radar. The calls are recorded with a sensitive microphone and analyzed with a computer program that identifies the various bird species by their call echoes. The photo shows the computer tracking of night migration calls.
(Courtesy: Adiv Gal)

Voice analysis allows migration magnitude to be studied according to the hours of the night and the various migration days.
(Courtesy: Adiv Gal)

By studying the relation between weather and bird migration in depth with the help of radar, we will truly be able to enter the third millennium in the field of flight safety. A regional radar network can also be of advantage in the developing field of ecotourism. Nature lovers will be able to receive real-time information on where to watch migrating birds and the theme can be further developed on a regional basis. Computer communications will allow the migration picture to be received on television. A tourist can turn on his TV set in the morning, and decide where he or she wants to watch migration that day, or on slow days or days with no migration, spend the time at an archeological site instead.

Schools too will be able to receive meteorological and migration data via the Internet. The students will thus be able to study one of the most fascinating of natural phenomena as well as communicating with other schools all over the world on the subject, and all this in real time. The Latrun Center has also initiated acoustic research in cooperation with the Ornithological Laboratory at Cornell University in the USA. Adiv Gal is in the final stages of his M.Sc. research in which he follows nocturnal bird migration with the Russian radar while recording the calls of the migrating species. With the help of sensitive microphones calls of night migrants can be recorded up to an altitude of 800 meters. The calls are then analyzed with an oscilloscope and compared to the radar data. This combination provides information on migration direction, velocity, intensity and altitude (see photos).

The rapid development of molecular biology in the past years has allowed migration research to spread to fields that had been difficult to study in the past. The population to which individual birds belong can today be identified by their DNA structure. These methods open new frontiers by enabling the determination of which migrating bird populations pass over Israel at what times, for example. Another possibility is the ability to examine whether a migration wave is composed of birds belonging to one population or several populations migrating together. By identifying the origin of passing populations one of the most interesting questions posed by migration can possibly be answered: does each population migrate for the shortest possible distance as far as optimal conditions are concerned? Or do the northernmost populations migrate the longest distances, to the southernmost end of their range, while populations breeding in the southern end of the range migrate only minimal distances, or possibly not at all.

The combination of laboratory and field work will lead to a better understanding of the water and energy regime of migrating birds, and how they face difficulties such as desert or sea crossings. Migration research results have several practical applications such as using the data gathered for managing the population size of

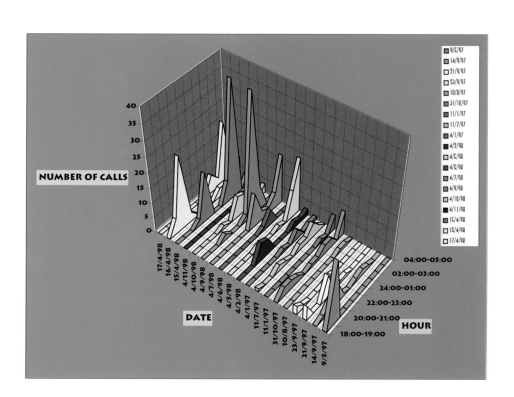

238

endangered birds or for reducing damage caused by migrants, such as pelicans, to agriculture as they pass over Israel. There are several cases of sharp conflict between agriculture and migrating birds in Israel and one is the damage caused by migrating flocks stopping over to rest and feed. A single White Pelican eats an average of 1200 grams of fish a day; a flock 2000 strong, landing to feed, can finish off 2.4 tons of fish just for "supper"! Another case is the problem with Cormorants that have started overwintering in Israel in numbers reaching 10,000 during the past few years. The average cormorant eats a "mere" 300 grams of fish daily, but when this occurs during four months out of every year, the damage becomes significant. Not only water birds cause problems to farmers: about 20,000 Common Crane winter in the Hula Valley and another 5,000 or so in the Coastal Plain and in the western Negev, feeding mainly on chickpeas and peanuts. On the other hand, the sight of 20,000 cranes gathering to roost each evening is breathtaking and has tremendous tourist potential.

D. The Center at Latrun - Migration, a First Rate Educational Tool

The Society for the Protection of Nature in Israel is building a unique educational complex, unlike any other in the world, in cooperation with the Armored Corps Memorial at Latrun. The complex will include a Field Study Center, a fifty-room hostel, an auditorium and interactive museum that will provide a visual presentation of Israel's unique location at the junction of three continents. Students and adults will be able to study the amazing phenomenon of bird migration, through a combination of viewing the radar screen, using the computer network for tracking birds with satellite transmitters attached and watching the birds through binoculars and telescope in the field. These activities will be part of a comprehensive program that will include excursions in the vicinity, emphasizing a wide variety of natural subjects as well as the history of the area, as is the custom in all 26 SPNI Field Study Centers in Israel.

With the help of the academic research institute to be established by Tel-Aviv University, students will be able to use data gathered over the past two decades by the academic community. This will provide them with the opportunity to do serious personal projects on bird migration, taking advantage of existing data.

During the past decade the Israeli Ministry of Education and Culture has developed a major project to advance scientific and technological education. The program is called "Tomorrow 98" and its stated goal is that every Israeli child will have free access to a computer and the basic knowledge to use it. The SPNI and Tel-Aviv University developed a curriculum on bird migration as part of this project - "Migrating Birds Know No Boundaries" - that is also the motto of the center being built at Latrun. The web site of "Migrating Birds Know no Boundaries" is:

http://www.birds.org.il

The curriculum is multidisciplinary, combining themes from biology, geography, physics and computer sciences. Participating students can use the Internet to follow the movements of migrating storks, vultures and cranes with satellite telemetry in real time, from their schools. While studying bird migration, the students can also use the Internet to receive weather data and see how they affect migration. The information gathered is used to establish a database at the participating school. The students complement the data gathered by computer with field trips to watch migration. They will communicate and share data and experiences with students in other schools doing the same work. The program is planned to work on three levels: Israel, the Middle East and the world. The program has already been successfully implemented in 40 different schools all over the country. Among the schools participating are several from the Arab sector, as well as the American School at Kfar Shmaryahu attended by the diplomatic community children.

עזרו לנו להציל את הבז האדום בירושלים!

חברת החשמל

Only 350 Lesser Kestrel pairs still nest in Israel of the 3500 that bred here 50 years ago. About 130 pairs nest in Jerusalem. We developed an educational program in which nest boxes were attached to houses to attract Lesser Kestrels. (Photo: Yossi Eshbol)

Lesser Kestrels nest in a nesting box in Jerusalem. (Photo: Gil'ad Liban)

Portrait of an Egyptian Vulture
(Photo: Yossi Eshbol - SPNI collection)

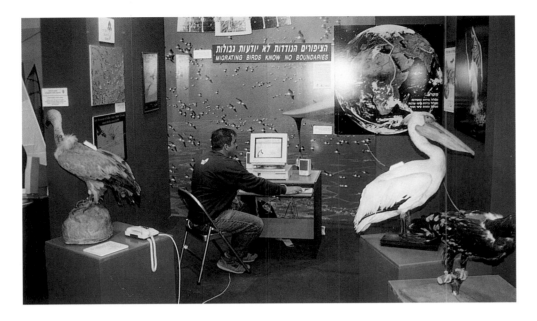

At the "Education 2000" exhibition in Jerusalem (31.12.95-12.1.96), in memory of the late Yitzhak Rabin, we presented our project in which students follow bird migration via satellite and computer communications.

Yossi Leshem explains the new project to Mrs. Leah Rabin, Rabin's sister Rachel and Prof. Amnon Rubinstein, the Minister of Education, At the "Education 2000" exhibition in Jerusalem.

Teachers learning about "Migrating Birds Know No Boundaries", an educational computer program for studying bird migration developed by the Latrun center in cooperation with the Israel Ministry of Education.

Mr. Ehud Olmert, Mayor of Jerusalem, was given the honor of attaching the first nest box for Lesser Kestrels.
He was raised with one of the Israel Electric Corporation cranes. This nest box was the first occupied by a pair
of Lesser Kestrels (as shown on page 239).
(Upper photo: Yossi Leshem)

A video camera was set up in one of the nests that allowed the nesting Lesser Kestrels to be observed in
real-time on our Internet site and on a screen set up on one of the Jerusalem streets. The screen attracted many
people who came to "peek" into the bird's bedroom. This project is funded by Charles and Andrea Bronfman
(CRB Foundation).
(Lower photo: Yossi Leshem)

E. Migrating Birds Play a Leading Role in the Middle East Peace Process

The unique location of Israel and the Palestinian Authority (PA) at the junction of three continents has made it the focus of political strife for many years, but also what made it a "bottleneck" and crossroads for bird migration second to almost no other site in the world. Birds migrating from Europe to Africa and back again fly over Lebanon, Jordan, Israel and the Palestinian Authority and through Egypt to Africa.

1994 and1995 were good years for peace in the Middle East. In the wake of the peace process, in 1997, the Society for the Protection of Nature in Israel (SPNI) and Tel-Aviv University initiated new relations with our Palestinian neighbors. The Children for the Protection of Nature in Palestine (CPNP), a Palestinian NGO, established an Environmental Education Center at the Lutheran school Thalita Kumi in Bet Jalla, west of Bethlehem, the first of its kind in the PA. These two new centers, in Latrun and Bet Jalla are developing an interdisciplinary project that will be linked to the peace process and bird migration. The plan calls for developing "twin centers" to promote themes related to bird migration on four levels: education, research, ecotourism and conservation. It is our hope that these themes will bring people together regardless of political barriers and help the peace process progress.

CPNP is a non-profit organization with a mission to promote peace and coexistence in the Middle East. It utilizes the theme of environmental action to encourage meaningful relations between youth who by working together across cultural boundaries can demonstrate the power and potential of partnership in addressing environmental challenges.

Thalita Kumi in Bet Jalla, has been chosen as the site for the center for several reasons: its varied natural surroundings, its proximity to both the Mediterranean and Dead Seas and its ideal facilities, spacious premises and laboratories.

The large amount of information and data gathered on bird migration over the past two decades, coupled with the unique geographical location of the PA and Israel present a singular opportunity for these two bird migration research centers. They can use the potential for interdisciplinary activity different fields to help promote additional ties between the countries of the Middle East as an important tool to advance the peace process in this sensitive region.

The initial idea is to develop "sister" stations where the CPNP station will play a leading role as the "twin sister" station to Latrun. The leading NGO in Jordan, the Royal Society for the Conservation of Nature (RSCN) has also agreed to join. If the peace process advances the hope is that more countries in the Middle East will join the project, under the title: Migrating Birds Know No Boundaries. This initiative was developed jointly by Yossi Leshem and Imad Atrash, CPNP director, a resident of Bet Sahour, east of Bethlehem, who is an educator and enthusiastic nature lover who established 50 nature groups for Palestinian youth in the West Bank.

The American Vice-President Mr. Al Gore visited Israel twice in March 1995 and January 1996. On both visits Yossi Leshem presented his project that combines three themes close to Mr. Gore's heart: environmental protection, education and computers. The Vice-President initiated the GLOBE program with the aim of bringing environmental protection into the home of students all over the world through computers. Mr. Gore was very enthusiastic about the possibility of promoting the subject via migrating birds with an emphasis on cooperation between Jordanians, Israelis and Palestinians, and expressed interest and his personal support for the plan. The United States Government then approved a sum of one million dollars via USAID-MERC to develop the link between Israelis, Palestinians and Jordanians and educational and scientific cooperation between them.

Two advanced computer classrooms were set up at the centers in Latrun and Thalita Kumi to train teachers and students how to use the internet to follow birds with transmitters attached. The aim of the program was for the Palestinian and Israeli children to communicate initially via computers and eventually to go out on joint birdwatching excursions. Each Israeli school would "adopt" a corresponding Palestinian school so the migrating birds would serve as a bridge between the people of the

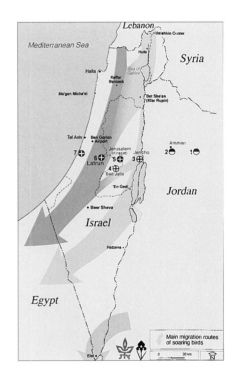

Cross-section of Israel-Jordan from Tel-Aviv to Amman illustrating the two main migration routes of soaring birds over Israel and the Palestinian Authority.
Legend:
☛ Proposed Jordanian migration research and education centers (RSCN).
⊕ Proposed Palestinian migration research and education centers (CPN-PIES).
● Proposed Israeli migration research and education centers (SPNI & TAU).
(Drawing: Vered Shatil)

243

Moshe Yanai, EMC [2] Vice-President, and his wife Racheli, at the joint Israeli-Palestinian ceremony at the EMC [2] offices in Tel-Aviv, Israel, to promote cooperation and the establishment of a joint Israeli-Palestinian database and to advance the computerization of the satellite project.
(Photo: Adiv Gal)

region. The first joint excursions to the Bet She'an and Hula Valleys, have already been successfully completed. In 1999 the Jordanians will also join the program led by the Royal Society for Conservation of Nature (RSCN), the largest NGO in Jordan. This organization, whose honorary President is Queen Noor, has 500 nature groups, several of which will have ties to the joint Israeli-Palestinian venture.

In September 1997 the International Center for the Study of Bird Migration at Latrun organized an international seminar in which representatives of 25 countries from five continents participated. The seminar's purpose was to advance educational and scientific cooperation and particularly to develop the internet program into a global program that countries all along the migration route would be able to join and participate in. Birdlife International, a leading ornithological society, is considering taking part in this project as well.

In 1995-1996 we presented our ideas to Mr. Shimon Peres, when he was Foreign Minister and later Prime Minister, and he was very impressed by the idea and its powerful potential. Mr. Peres, who is now President of the Peres Center for Peace, has agreed to be Honorary Chairman of the project in the Middle East.

Regional cooperation focuses not only on education, but also on developing joint research on the subject of migration. A network of weather and bird radars will be set up at key points in the Middle East and will feed data into a central database for Israel, the PA and Jordan. This information will enable us to make huge strides in understanding bird migration, by allowing real-time tracking of bird concentration movements.

Amir Balaban, coordinator of the ringing station in the Knesset garden ringing a songbird with Simon Awad, Michael Farhoud and Riad Abu-Sa'ada with the purpose of establishing a Palestinian ringing station in the near future in Bet Jalla and eventually in Jordan.
(Photo: Yossi Leshem)

244

Palestinian children watching migrating storks with Israeli children from the Beth She'an Valley as part of the cooperative program.
(Photo: Yossi Leshem)

The ground observer network that is spread across Israel from the Mediterranean coast to the Rift Valley during migratory seasons will be expanded to include Palestinians and Jordanians. In this manner we can establish a 150-km wide birdwatching front whose observations will be recorded on a single database. EMC2, a leading data storage company in Boston, has sponsored the development of a regional database on bird migration for the Latrun project, which in its second stage will include the Jordanian and Palestinian data.

The "twin" stations at Latrun and Thalita Kumi are also developing joint research on night migration in cooperation with the Cornell Univesity Laboratory of Ornithology for recording and doing computer analysis of nocturnal migrant calls. Two graduate students, Simon Awad from the PA and Adiv Gal from Israel, have begun studying the subject together in the Rose Garden adjacent to the Israeli Knesset (parliament) where an Israeli team has been ringing birds for the last ten years. In 1999 the first Palestinian ringing station will be established at Thalita Kumi and it will work with the Israeli station in Jerusalem, as part of the joint project. This is the first time ever that Palestinian and Jordanian bird ringers will be using their own rings. By the year 2000 a network of six stations - 2 Israeli, 2 Palestinian and 2 Jordanian - will be operating from the Mediterranean coast to the Jordanian Desert (see map).

April 28, 1998: The opening ceremony of the CPNP environmental center at the Talitha Kumi School in Bet Jalla, west of Bethlehem. Left to right: The Palestinian Minister of the Environment, Dr. Sultan Sufian and Dr. Yossi Leshem releasing a ringed male Kestrel. Imad Atrash, director of the CPNP is watching on the right. The CPNP center at Bet Jalla will be the "twin" center of the International Center for the Study of Bird Migration at Latrun in Israel, established by Tel-Aviv Unviersity and the SPNI.
(Photo: Adiv Gal)

245

The Bearded Vulture spreads its wings.
(Drawing: Trevor Boyer)

Pages 248-249:
Watching migrating birds in the field is part of the development of a system of joint research, tourism and flight
safety projects and an outstanding instrument for bringing Jews and their Arab neighbors together. In this photo
Jews and Arabs are watching migration together along the western axis in the Kfar-Kasem fields.
(Photo: Yossi Eshbol, SPNI)

Above: Professor Heinrich Mendelssohn and Azariya Alon, two of the founders of the SPNI, present Prime Minister Shimon Peres with the first copy of the Bearded Vulture poster. The Hebrew word "Peres" means Bearded Vulture. Mr. Peres changed his name from Perski to Peres while travelling in the Negev Desert with Professor Mendelssohn in 1944 and watching the "Peres" in flight.
(Upper photo: Zoom 77)

Yossi Leshem exhibiting the "Migrating Birds Know no Boundaries" project to Mr. Al Gore, Vice-President of the United States, during his visit to Israel. The themes of computers, education and conservation are very important to Mr. Gore, who was very enthusiastic about the Israeli project and its potential for international cooperation.
(Lower photo)

F. The Development of Local and Regional Ecotourism and Birdwatching

The economic potential of ecotourism, in particular birdwatching, is tremendous. Some 17 million birdwatchers belong to various ornithological societies the world over and many travel to distant lands with the sole purpose of seeing as many avian species as possible and large concentrations of migrating birds.

Within a period of two months one autumn, more than 35,000 people visited a raptor migration observation station established by the SPNI near Kfar Qassem (east of Tel-Aviv). A similar number visited the International Birdwatching Center in Eilat, where surveys, research and bird ringing (banding) are conducted daily. The potential for birdwatching tours in this area is unlimited and the development of several major birdwatching sites is planned in neighboring countries. Birdwatching tours covering Israel, the Palestinian Authority, Jordan and Egypt can then be developed, boosting bird-related tourism in these countries, as has occurred in Israel during the past two decades.

We have begun setting up a country-wide network of nine research and observation stations that will combine activities with students and the public on local and migrating birds with work by several field researchers. The Latrun Center will be the national focus for developing the network, so those tourists visiting Israel and interested in birds can begin or end their trip at the Latrun site, only a quarter of an hour away from Ben-Gurion International Airport. On-line information on where the best place to watch birds at this time of year will be available as well as literature and instructions necessary to reach roosting and migration sites.

In the early 1980's the SPNI led by Yossi Leshem initiated the International Birdwatching Center at Eilat (IBCE). The center is now a joint association of the SPNI, the Israel Nature Reserves Authority, the Jewish National Fund, the Eilat Municipality and the Ministry of Tourism and is directed by Dr. Reuven Yosef. A birdwatching trail has been developed in the fields north of the Gulf of Eilat, and there is research, survey and bird ringing activity. Eilat has become a Mecca for birdwatchers and an estimated 35,000 visit the IBCE yearly. At the Hatzeva Field Study Center in the Arava Valley, Professor Amotz Zahavi from Tel-Aviv University, who has been studying the behavior of Arabian Babblers, a communally nesting species, for three decades, established a research station that can host up to 12 researchers. At Sede Boqer in the Negev Highlands, the field study center works alongside the Ben-Gurion University Institute for Desert Research. The Sede Boqer Academy is located above the Nahal Tsin cliffs, where Griffon Vultures nest and many other desert birds are active. A major migration route exists in the area but although the region has great potential for birders it has not been developed yet.

In Jerusalem, the SPNI and the Biblical Zoo have set up a bird ringing (banding) station in the gardens adjacent to the Knesset (Israel's parliament), one of the prominent green spots in the heart of the capital, where many songbirds reside and stopover for a rest during migration. The ringing station, under the auspices of the Knesset Speaker, will attract many tourists visiting the Knesset and is already open to students from Jerusalem schools.

As a result of the diminishing economic importance of agriculture, many kibbutzim are looking for alternative sources of income, and tourism is one of them. Kibbutz Kfar Ruppin, in the northern Bet She'an Valley, a veritable paradise for wintering birds, and located along a major migration route in the Rift Valley, is now a full fledged member of this network. The kibbutz has prepared 20 rooms to accommodate birdwatchers, as well as paying the salary for a full time bird ringer and for a project manager who works in close cooperation with the SPNI Ornithology Center.

The Hula Valley was once a marsh land of global importance. The marshes were drained after the State of Israel arose, despite efforts of a group of concerned citizens, whose activity led to the establishment of the Society for the Protection of Nature in Israel in 1953. In 1995, part of the area was flooded to develop a base for nature tourism, with the flooded area planned to be the focus for ornithological activity. Dan Alon, who heads the Israel Ornithological Center, is doing a field research on

Over 100,000 bird lovers visit northern Germany to watch Crane migration during three weeks. In the Hula Valley 20,000 cranes winter for five and a half months each year and can be a major attraction for birdwatchers from the entire world.
(Photo: Yossi Leshem)

The winning combination of a migration focal point for hundreds of millions of birds and warm sun most of the
year is perfect for developing ecotourism in general and birdwatching in particular.
(Photo: Yossi Leshem)

March 23, 1998: Speaker of the Knesset Mr. Dan Tichon releases a Kestrel at the inauguration of the Jerusalem Bird Ringing Station in the Knesset Garden in Jerusalem.
(Upper photo: Zoom 77)

The State of Israel allotted one and a half acres in the Rose Garden adjacent to the Knesset for the establishment of a ringing station from migrating birds. The station focuses on a combination of research and guiding students and tourists. To the best of our knowledge this is the first parliament in the world to have a permanent ringing station in its grounds.
(Lower photo: Yossi Leshem)

More than 30,000 soldiers and civilians participated in the Latrun Walk in spring 1997. This lieutenant, a new immigrant from Ehtiopia, is leading a group of soldiers on the walk.
(Photo: Yossi Leshem)

the 20,000 wintering cranes in the area that is funded by Euronatur, a German fund. Mr. Jurgen Weber, President of Lufthansa, visited the Latrun Center and Thalita Kumi in 1998. Lufthansa's logo is a crane in flight, and Mr. Weber decided to sponsor the crane project in the Hula Valley, provide satellite transmitters and help develop educational cooperation with the Palestinians.

Another area where agriculture and tourism coexist is near the Ma'agan Mikhael Field Study Center, on the Carmel coast, where there is a large concentration of fish ponds, with great potential for watching waterfowl, waders and other birds.

At this time there are several proposals for establishing bird observatories in the area of the Palestinian Authority that would work in cooperation with Israel, complementing the data gathered by the Israeli observatories. Two such stations are already planned, one in the town of Bet Jalla, at the Thalita Kumi school and another in Jericho, in the heart of the migration route. Israeli-Palestinian cooperation can be the beginning of a network that would eventually include Jordan, Egypt, and hopefully as peace progresses, other Middle Eastern countries. We believe nature and bird lovers from Europe and North America will be eager to take advantage of joint birdwatching packages to Israel, Jordan and the Palestinian Authority.

Another subject that will be studied in this framework is the conservation of migrating birds and their roosting areas. Systematic research on migrating birds conservation issues will add to our knowledge of migration and preferred roosting and wintering areas. Recommendations based on this data will be passed on to relevant people and governments concerning sensitive and threatened areas in need of protection. The increasing popularity of ecotourism will provide a solid economic basis for these recommendations.

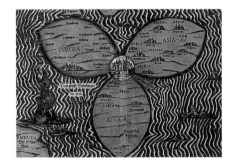

The Banting Map, drawn in 1851 in Hanover, Germany, whose symbol is a cloverleaf. The map was drawn as a cloverleaf with one continent on each of the three leaves and Jerusalem and the Middle East at the junction of three continents. The drawing illustrates excellently why migrating birds avoid crossing the sea and converge over Israel.

Thousands of soldiers have seen the exhibit on birds of prey and their conservation.
(Photo: Israel Sun)

253

Above: January 10 1997, General John Shalikashvili, Chairman of the US Joint Chiefs of Staff visiting Latrun, Israel and learning about the new bird migration center there and the idea of developing a network of bird and weather radars in cooperation with Israel, Jordan, Turkey and the US Air Force. (Right to left: Major General Yoram Yair, Dr. Yossi Leshem, General Shalikashvili and Major General Amos Malka.

G. Information and Public Activity

The Latrun Center is active in education, research, flight safety and promoting bird-related tourism, while at the same time investing effort in exposing the public at large to this activity. The aim of these endeavors is to bring this theme to more and more people in Israel and abroad that will then be more closely involved in nature and bird conservation. The Center staff lecture extensively within the school system and to the public at large as well as in the Israel Defense Forces, particularly in the IAF.

The International Center for the Study of Bird Migration and the Armored Corps Association hold the "Latrun Walk" every year in spring. Some 25,000 people walk out from Latrun enjoying nature and bird migration in the area and end their day in the Latrun Amphitheater in the presence of the President or one of the senior government ministers. During the day bird migration is manifested by exhibitions, guided birdwatching tours, talks and other activities.

Hundreds of thousands of copies of this phone card dedicated to the satellite-telemetry migration study with the title of the Latrun center and "Migrating Birds Know No Boundaries" were distributed.

The Center in conjunction with the SPNI and the Israel Ornithology Center organizes study days that attract hundreds of nature lovers and publish the "Torgos" a journal for birdwatchers in Israel. Every year in a joint venture with the Israel Government Company for Medals and Coins, the Israel Philatelic Service and the Unicover Company in the United States, a conservation stamp with one of the migrating duck species and a first-day cover are published along with a postal stamp and gold and silver medals. Phone cards have been produced with the Bezeq Telecommunications Co. and private companies and many articles on migration appear in the media making this a subject constantly in the public mind.

Independence Day, 1992. The Ben-Gurion International Airport was closed and about 300,000 people came to see the aerial show. The subject of birdwatching and migration research was exhibited on a large area and visited by many people and included the vehicle with 2 radars for studying night migration at the front of the photo and the motorized glider in the background.
(Photo: Yossi Leshem)

254